understanding

ALL SUCCESS IS ATTAINED BY IT

GODLY WRITES PUBLISHING
ORANGEBURG, SC

SHANE WALL

Published by:
Godly Writes Publishing
P. O. Box 2005
Orangeburg SC 29116-2005

Unless otherwise noted, Scripture quotations taken from the Amplified® Bible, Copyright © 1954, 1958, 1962, 1964, 1965, 1987 by The Lockman Foundation
Used by permission. www.lockman.org

Scripture quotations marked KJV are taken from the King James Version of the Bible.
Public Domain.

UNDERSTANDING — ALL SUCCESS IS ATTAINED BY IT
ISBN 10: 0-9704093-0-3
ISBN 13: 978-0-9704093-0-0

LIBRARY OF CONGRESS CONTROL NUMBER: 2014909602

COVER DESIGN BY GREG JACKSON, THINKPEN DESIGN

10 9 8 7 6 5 4 3

FOR WORLDWIDE DISTRIBUTION, PRINTED IN THE U.S.A.

WWW.UNDERSTANDINGNOW.COM

DEDICATION

This book is dedicated to my awesome church family, The Feast of the Lord.

Your growth in God has inspired me to continue teaching the Word of God with all I have and will have for His glory! I love each of you so very much!

ACKNOWLEDGEMENTS

The #1 editing team in the world:
David C. Marshall, Jr. — davidhelp.me
Keith Carroll — christianliteraryagent.com
Jordone Branch — jordonewrites.com
Eddie Massey, III
G. Miki Hayden

My wife, Jasmyne
My father, Hoover Wall

Pastor Hayward Jean and family
The Feast of the Lord family
The Church FM (Fellowship Ministry)

TABLE OF CONTENTS

INTRODUCTION

When I mentioned to a number of people that I was writing a book on understanding, I began noticing that many of them responded by displaying the same facial expression: a look of wonder and contemplation. I knew the exact thought they pondered before they even spoke.

They'd say, "Understanding...the *Bible*? Understanding... *what*?"

I'd just smile and say, "No, just *understanding*."

"How in the world can you find enough information to write a whole book on such an abstract subject as *understanding*?"

I shared with them a brief revelation concerning the topic, and afterward, the proverbial light bulb of understanding lit up over their heads.

"Ah! I get it now...wow!"

I came to expect these and similar types of initial responses as I presented the "understanding" message. To be honest, I was myself pleasantly surprised when the Holy Spirit revealed such an untouched theme to me. Early in my exploration of the subject, I heard this comment: "Just when you thought every major topic in the Bible had been preached, written about, discussed and/or published on, God unveils yet another."

Even a pastor friend of mine remarked about *understanding*, saying, "I've been to church every week of my life and have ministered in over 60 countries, but I've never even heard *one* sermon on *understanding*."

I myself am 45 years old, and having been a church-goer since infancy, I've attended thousands of church services. At no time had I ever considered *understanding* to be a prime issue to teach or preach about because it simply wasn't a popular theme that I'd heard ministers share. I did know that the Bible declares, "... in all thy getting get understanding." (Proverbs 4:7, KJV) I had also heard several preachers say that we are not to lean to our *own* understanding. (Proverbs 3:5) That was about the extent of my knowledge concerning *understanding*.

What subjects in life do you deem to be major? Which valued reference would you elect to use that would support your choices?

The Holy Bible is a highly recognized resource that presents vital subject matters and answers to everyday problems in our lives. The 2013 State of the Bible report produced by the American Bible Society reveals that a majority of Americans own a Bible and believe what the Bible says. An impressive 88 percent own a Bible, 80 percent say the Bible is sacred and 61 percent wish they read it more often.

These statistics make overwhelmingly clear why even across religious divides, the Holy Bible is the number one bestselling book of all time. Undoubtedly, its pages include unmatched wisdom and advice for dealing with all of life's problems.

The Sacred Scriptures, another term used when referencing the Bible, are paramount. This is the literal Word of God. Psalm 138:2 even declares that God has magnified His Word above all

His name, meaning, if God Himself disobeyed even one part of His own Word, He could no longer be enthroned as King of the Universe.

With that in mind, contextually speaking, certain topics are considered important because of the way they're introduced or mentioned in the Bible. The subject of *understanding* has equal, if not greater importance alongside many other points of attention in God's Word.

Themes such as faith, love, wisdom, righteousness and healing are dwelt on extensively in the Scriptures. We find these especially important because of how the verses tend to command our focus when they're discussed. Therefore, since Proverbs 4:7, KJV, relates that in all we get, we need to get understanding, the attention bestowed on understanding reveals its high level of importance.

In the King James Version of the Holy Bible, the word *understand* appears 91 times. The word *understandest* appears four times; the word *understandeth* appears 11 times. The word *understanding* appears 160 times, and the word *understood* appears 37 times. That's a total of 303 times, which is more than the words joy, grace and believe can be found, inclusive of their derivatives.

Due to the fact that *understanding* is so frequently mentioned in the Bible, I wanted to conduct a search before titling this book. I was instructed years ago that before deciding on a book's title, searching for that title at amazon.com and other similar sites is wise.

My search yielded a startling discovery. I couldn't find a single book entitled *Understanding* or any other title discussing only this subject.

I used the Holy Bible as the sole, written resource to build material for this message of *understanding*. The Holy Spirit, the only other Source of information I've accessed for this project, gave me many revelations concerning *understanding*, and the knowledge offered me fills this book's pages.

The Holy Spirit also shared with me that understanding brings success. He explained that success is the continual occurrence that comes about when we strive through understanding to fulfill our life's mission on this Earth.

When God created our lives, He didn't ask Himself, "What am I going to do with this child?" My studies have led me to conclude that God creates a purpose, and at the same time, He creates an individual to fulfill that purpose. I believe the Lord then places that individual in a set of intentional events called *life*. As we journey through life, purpose reveals the assignment that God expects to be faithfully executed until completion. *The working toward that end* is true success.

Success must first begin in us before it can be presented *by* us. *Understanding* applies a molding effect on our minds and character, shaping us into that which God desires for us to become, resulting in imminent success.

As you read the remaining pages of this book, allow the Holy Spirit to impart *understanding* into your heart. Then you will have satisfied the prerequisite for experiencing all the success God has made available to you.

CHAPTER 1
WHAT IS UNDERSTANDING?

My mother died unexpectedly in September of 2008. The entire ordeal was hard for me to grasp emotionally. Later, after she was taken to the emergency room and pronounced, I had a few minutes with her alone, a time that sticks out vividly for me.

I remember being at the foot of my mother's bed. I hit the bottom of her feet with my hands and said, "Get up in Jesus' name!" Immediately after the words emerged from my mouth, a strong feeling came over me. I felt as if electricity was flowing through every vein and artery in my body. I thought to myself, *Could this sensation be the power of God? Is this evidence that I'm about to see a miracle?* The feeling was intense enough for me to believe that my mother was about to be raised from the dead, right before my eyes.

I was so moved by God's electrifying presence that I looked directly at my mother's face, expecting her to open her eyes and breathe. But she didn't. As her body remained in its lifeless state, I felt a wave of embarrassing disappointment; tears began to well up in my eyes.

My oldest sister and a few other people came into the room. Ashamed and saddened at my defeat, I moved to a side wall and leaned on a counter. God spoke to me there and said verbatim, "I heard you, but that's not what I wanted to do."

I had mixed emotions at that point, very mixed emotions. Despite the confusion those feelings caused, the Lord's voice allowed me to confirm as truths a couple of notions. One was that my mother wasn't going to receive the miracle of being raised from the dead. The other was that God's timing was for her to leave.

Psalm 111:10 declares that when we get good understanding in our lives, our praise of Him will endure forever. My praise endured through this very tough time because I received God's own perception of that event. If I hadn't received God's understanding so I could make it my own, I would still be wondering if my mother died before her time.

Life has a way of presenting some peculiar situations that cause us to wonder. Understanding, however, replaces wonder—though grabbing hold of this can be a challenging sport of its own.

Understanding is essential to completing each everyday activity. Whether you're drinking a glass of water or managing a Fortune 500 company, you need to have understanding in order to carry out your tasks.

Information can give birth to understanding, just as it did when God told me that my mother's demise was His will. That settled all the questions that were in my mind.

Ask a man what understanding he has about taking care of a family and he will give you knowledge. Ask a mother what understanding she has about giving birth to a child, and she will give you knowledge. Ask a multimillionaire what understanding she has about producing wealth, and she will give you knowledge. Receiving knowledge enables us to gain *understanding*.

The primary reason most of us don't understand certain ordeals in our lives is simply because we have yet to receive enough knowledge to cancel our bewilderment. When we have trouble accepting that particular events have happened to us, instead of using the Word of God to move past these circumstances, we put ourselves in a state of uncertainty that leaves us baffled.

In life we face many problems needing resolution. Frequently, we quickly find ourselves deciding that the situation is too challenging for us to conquer.

If we would be honest with ourselves, we would confess that we often give up on solving these dilemmas far too quickly. Usually, a lack of understanding is at the base of our surrender to the difficulty. Not only are we adding disappointment to our lives by simply capitulating, but we also forfeit the opportunity to advance our understanding.

Most of us retreat from dealing with troublesome situations because our past experiences have convinced us that we're much weaker than the problem. This notion may be true, but our inability was only based on what we understood at the time.

What frustrated me most about my mother's death was not that she died so abruptly, but rather that she refused to go to the hospital to receive the proper care. She had been sick for about a week prior to her death, and that whole week was a process of back and forth arguing about the severity of her condition.

"I only have a common cold," she would reiterate in a firm tone each time a member of my family tried to convince her otherwise.

Somehow I knew her illness was more than just an ordinary ailment. I could feel the distress creeping into my bones as she continued to exclaim what we all knew was wrong. That I knew better, but still felt so helpless, irritated me. As I watched her breathe in pain from an apparent soreness in her clavicle, I could feel the anger boiling inside of me because she declined the medical care I knew she needed.

I offered to take her to the hospital or call for an ambulance. She refused both. I just could not fathom why she wouldn't let me help her.

Not until after she died was I able to understand why she didn't want medical attention. Although she never said so out loud, I sincerely believe that she knew her time of death was close. She wanted to die at home in peace, and that she did.

I would have been in much greater anguish had I convinced her to go to the hospital. If she'd died in the hospital only because I forced her to be there, I would have neglected to fulfill her unspoken desire. She wanted to rest in her own bed and go to Heaven from there.

I felt an overwhelming sense of peace in my heart as I embraced this revelation. My frustration with her stark rejection ended when I understood her reasoning.

What is frustrating *your* life right now? Could it be that understanding is waiting to rescue you, saving you from this (unnecessary) exasperation? Where then is your understanding? How do you get it? What happens afterward?

The following pages of this book will help you determine, define, and destroy the major and minor encumbrances that prevent understanding. You may have spent years attempting to comprehend the loss of your marriage, job, or any other relationship—for example. Receiving truth on issues like these will reward you with achieving your life's goals and give you peace of mind to boot.

The following scripture, for one, arouses much conviction. It is the textual, focal point of this book's message:

> *Wisdom is the principal thing; therefore get wisdom: and with all thy getting get understanding.*
>
> Proverbs 4:7, KJV

This scripture isn't shy in demanding that definite attention be given to understanding. There's no doubting here that *wisdom* is indeed the principal quality required for understanding one's life. The definition of *understanding* that I have formulated is *revealed insight.* On the other hand, wisdom is defined as *the quality of having experience, knowledge, and good judgment.*

An observer may call a brilliant scientist wise beyond measure. While the scientist may be full of wisdom, understanding is the quality that gives his research true success. Because he understands science, his ability to research can give rise to many astounding discoveries. Understanding is the force that takes our gifts, abilities, and talents to transform them into practical tools. Even though the scientist may have wisdom, understanding is the quality that makes the observer really discerning.

We can say that wisdom causes us to know, while understanding enables us to act. Pondering on such a thought shows its truth, particularly when examined in the light of the following scripture:

> *Give me understanding, and I shall keep thy law; yea, I shall observe it with my whole heart.*
>
> Psalm 119:34, KJV

Keeping the Law of God refers to being obedient to whatever God says—taking action (whether exterior or interior). Observing His Law with our entire heart also refers to our obedience but is further referenced by our passion and drive to know and to act on all He has commanded.

The psalmist who wrote this verse felt his life was void of the important component necessary for him to successfully complete what he desired to do. His request to God was not to help him be obedient, nor was it to help his whole heart be toward God's Word. His wise request was for the attribute he needed to fulfill those desired tasks. He needed *understanding*.

God longs to give us understanding, *His* understanding. Our unwillingness to trustingly believe Him can interrupt or cancel His gift of understanding.

If we have understanding, God is the One responsible for giving us the knowledge that brings it.

> *He changes the times and the seasons; He removes kings and sets up kings. He gives wisdom to the wise and knowledge to those who have understanding!*
>
> Daniel 2:21

The wise are wise because God gave them wisdom. Those who understand do so because God first gave them knowledge.

If I could interview Abraham, Moses, Noah, or any other major Bible character, I'd ask, "What is understanding?" Having myself gathered much knowledge from God's most Holy Word, I sincerely believe in my heart their response would be, "Every Word that God speaks is truth. Therefore, understanding is whatever God *speaks*."

How then do we get understanding from God? We must wholeheartedly believe what He says. *Whatever* God says *is* the understanding.

No added thoughts to what God says are necessary because He has already invested all the thought needed into what He declares. Any additional thoughts, considerations, or wonderings concerning what He speaks are the forbidden acts of leaning toward our own understanding.

> *Trust in the Lord with all thine heart; and*
> *lean not unto thine own understanding.*
> Proverbs 3:5, KJV

If you want to get understanding from God, believe that what He says is correct and critical to your learning. Doubting Him, just because what you believe is different, will prevent you from getting His understanding.

Everyone wants success. The problem is not that other people hinder us from achieving success in life nor is the problem the fact that money isn't freely accessible to us. The *real* problem that we have is getting understanding, because understanding is the element that attracts success into our lives.

Understanding can take us to notable places in life. Understanding is attractive, respected, honored, and is even envied.

But there is one thing that understanding is not. It is not highly sought after.

CHAPTER 2
SEEKING UNDERSTANDING

Do you remember how peppy jingles used to be? Our favorite brands would use those short songs to grab people's attention. A couple of my favorites were, "I like the Sprite in you" and, "The best part of waking up is Folgers in your cup."

In my teen years I discovered a knack for writing jingles. I badly wanted to know how to break into the jingle business, but what I learned was quite discouraging. Advertising agencies hired jingle houses to produce the songs for their commercials, but jingle houses didn't accept unsolicited jingles.

Determined to break through this brass ceiling, I looked for opportunities to submit a jingle to a local company. My mother sold insurance for Primerica back when it was still AL Williams Insurance Company. One day, I asked the manager of the local office about writing a jingle for the company. He gave me the address where I could send whatever I came up with.

I wrote the lyrics and composed the tune for a 60-second jingle and sent that with a letter to the company's home office. My talented cousin Michael Ross helped by supplying the musical accompaniment for my little song. It wasn't long before a blue envelope from the company arrived in the mail. My parents woke me up that morning, grinning from ear to ear.

I opened the envelope, my hands trembling, and read it aloud.

Dear Shane,

Thank you for sending your jingle to us. This is an excellent representation of our company, and we'd love to use it for our employee satellite broadcasts. Unfortunately, since this is for an internal channel, we're unable to provide you with compensation should you release the jingle to us.

They wanted me to sign a form stating that the company wouldn't owe me any money if they used the jingle. I signed and mailed it back to them. They used the jingle on their international, interoffice, satellite network for the pleasure of tens of thousands of their executives and representatives. This notoriety opened doors for me to write jingles for a couple of local companies.

In those days, state-to-state calls were charged by the minute. I made so many calls trying to pursue understanding and dive further into the jingle business that my parents' monthly phone bill ran over $300. A talk-show radio host suggested that I needed to travel to a larger city where the jingle houses were located and there knock on doors. My funds, though, weren't supportive of that suggestion.

I did my best, but then ended my pursuit of making it big in the music portion of the advertising business. My failure wasn't at all because I was lazy, but because a career writing jingles wasn't really my dream. Writing these songs was just a hobby that I thought would make me famous and wealthy one day. My actual dream was to preach everywhere I could to save souls for God.

> *Many plans are in a man's mind, but it is the*
> *Lord's purpose for him that will stand.*
>   Proverbs 19:21

I worked passionately to get understanding about the jingle business. I purchased books and made phone calls to all the places I could think of. I searched to find the right information that would make me a great success.

What I found, though, was a greater understanding than just of the advertising industry. This understanding revealed my heart's true passion, which was stronger than my transitory desire to produce jingles for commercials. No matter the exact results, seeking whatever kind of understanding we desire seems to have the power to uncover who we really are.

We can find countless true stories of those who never stopped persevering in their quests to fulfill their missions on the earth. The reason the popular all-purpose cleaner is named Formula 409 is because two young Detroit scientists tried 408 formulas that failed to meet their expectation. They accomplished their goal because they sought after and then continuously applied the understanding that the right formula was their life's mission to create.

In my case, I don't feel guilty about quitting my pursuit of success in the jingle trade because it simply wasn't my life's purpose.

When our life's meaning is realized, that understanding is sewn into the very fiber of our existence. That consciousness opens our eyes, lifts our heads, and has us standing in firm confidence. Our state of being then transforms along the way from confidence to real enthusiasm.

Another observation that comes with the above is clear. We aren't just existing to take up space. Our lives have purposes here that we need to determine. Seeking for that specific understanding gives us a very targeted focus and fuels our drive toward fulfilling our destiny.

Every waking day dawns with a new opportunity to experience a wonderful state of *becoming*. We are now becoming what we are to be. My journey in regard to the jingle business didn't progress very smoothly, but the roadblocks I encountered were actually God's way of steering me to my real intended life's purpose.

Once you realize your life's distinctive purpose, an almost automatic response is to seek for the understanding of what that entails. We then must undertake a conscious effort to get the understanding needed. Quite frankly, we often need a deeper revelation of who we are to motivate us to seek for the understanding.

The aim of this chapter is to illustrate that *seeking* will, in fact, *give* you understanding. We now want to focus on Who provides that understanding: God.

He is the One Who has all Understanding. The One Who has it is the One Who will give it, and He is more than willing to give us understanding. He longs to give it to us, in fact. But as with all things we might want or need, we, ourselves, aren't to seek that understanding. We are to seek God. Those who seek Him desperately will never be disappointed in the results.

God looked down from heaven upon the children of men to see if there were any who understood, who sought (inquired after and desperately required) God.

Psalm 53:2

No one understands [no one intelligently discerns or comprehends]; no one seeks out God.

Romans 3:11

Evil men understand not judgment: but they that seek the Lord understand all things.

Proverbs 28:5, KJV

Seeking God naturally leads to understanding our lives from His perspective. This happens because seeking God allows us to show Him that He is the focus of our dependence, trust, and expectation. We do not seek humanity to get their understanding of our lives. We seek God for *His* understanding.

CHAPTER 3
WHAT IS GOD'S UNDERSTANDING?

When I was in school for respiratory therapy, I never enjoyed sitting through theory classes because they always required me to learn abstract, mind-numbing information. Theoretical classes were just not my cup of tea. I'm the kind of person who loves hands-on learning. If we're exploring electric circuits, I want a circuit board and soldering tools right in front of me. If I'm studying law, I'd better be in the courtroom observing tough cases and not behind the desk looking at files.

I loathed the classes in which the professor droned on for hours about professional bedside manners or detecting abnormal breathing patterns. As the class dragged along, my attention span would dwindle until I finally stepped into a patient's room to gather a blood sample.

I was great at drawing blood from arteries that no one else could seem to penetrate, but at a certain point in my clinical exercises, I realized that the lessons in theory actually helped me to develop my skills. As excited as I was to begin administering respiratory therapy, the engaging moments of drawing blood would have been a lot less exciting had I messed up. The theory taught me what I needed for the clinical setting.

Much as in the practice of respiratory therapy, we are faced with everyday situations that cause us to put our understanding of life into practice. Every day, we come into contact with people who will test us. They lie to us, cheat on us, and even steal from us.

Although it is man who disappoints us in these ways, when difficulties arise, we tend to rely on the advice of others instead of on the commands of God. But we have to be certain that those we trust to learn from are of God. Whose understanding you apply to your life determines whether you're taking a risk with man or following the plan of God. Your success in life is ultimately contingent upon which choice you decide to make. The importance of living according to God's will lies in the fact that He always understands our lives better than we do.

When you're faced with confusion about a circumstance in your life, it's always important to ask God how He desires you to see the matter before taking further steps. Too often, we take action before receiving God's unambiguous perception of a situation. In other words, before we do anything, we need to practice asking God the question: What is *Your* understanding concerning this matter?

As we learn from the following scripture, if your viewpoint is entirely reliant upon your trust and confidence in the Lord, you should have none left to be placed in anyone else—especially yourself.

> *Lean on, trust in, and be confident in the*
> *Lord with all your heart and mind and do not*
> *rely on your own insight or understanding.*
>
> Proverbs 3:5

Once you've given God your all, you will have nothing left to give to a devil. Placing your all in God means no amount of trust or confidence remains in any devil or man who can lead your faith astray. If a devil has used you, he was able to take advantage of a part of you that had not been given to God.

Whether from a parent teaching us the alphabet or the news reports we receive about government policies, we have acquired the human inclination to gather perspectives from sources other than ourselves. We've built up so many of our own social cues, tendencies, and best practices that we've become comfortable relying on our own senses to gain insight, instead of getting the insight directly from God.

The result of leaning on our own understanding is that many in the world have come to believe that *their* actions do not require a dependency on God's input in their lives. We have become accustomed to acting on our own impulses instead of seeking His knowledge.

Every situation is different, and God is the only One Who really knows the outcome. God wants to reveal to you what's truly going on in your life and what you should do in every circumstance, but you have to be willing to seek Him first.

> *In all your ways know, recognize, and acknowledge Him, and He will direct and make straight and plain your paths.*
>
> Proverbs 3:6

As we allow the Lord to continuously direct our paths, we're able to understand what God is like. Knowing God's tendencies and habits is a sure way of grasping how to apply His understanding to our lives.

But let him who glories glory in this: that he understands and knows Me [personally and practically, directly discerning and recognizing My character], I am the Lord, Who practices loving-kindness, judgment, and righteousness in the earth, for in these things I delight, says the Lord.

Jeremiah 9:24

As we analyze the previous scripture, it reveals how God desires us to understand Him. We discover that God views us in light of His own character traits. By noting the character of God in the verse above, we're able to predict how God is likely to react in certain situations. The characteristics of God are not only the attributes of His nature, but they are also the means by which He understands.

Let's examine the first characteristic of God, His Lordship. In Hebrew, the term *Lord* means owner. God owns everything (Psalms 24:1). He's the One Who created us and He knows everything about us. He also owns everyone—those who love us and those who hurt us. We should go directly to the Owner when we need understanding.

Although God is our Sole Proprietor, He gives us control over our lives. When difficulties arise, we have the choice of either listening to God or going our own ways. Our lack of understanding blocks us from having faith in what we can't see. Subsequently, His ultimate purpose is inhibited by our inability to let go of what control we think we have over our most troubling circumstances.

In reality, when God owns our lives, we don't control the situation. He does. But God doesn't barge into our lives. He wants to be invited in. After we invite Him, all we have to do is step back from the controls, and watch God steer the remaining course of our lives.

God isn't an evil and angry Lord. He is a Father, full of loving-kindness. In order to know Who God is, we must understand His *loving-kindness*, defined as His enduring grace, favor, and mercy toward us. To get understanding about a certain state of affairs, we must know that God always deals with us through these gracious gifts. Even when times are rough, God is still full of loving-kindness.

How many of us can say that we've been through something difficult in our lives? Being that we're still alive, it's safe to assume that God has brought us out of every single hardship that we've encountered. Why then do we worry when negative circumstances arise?

The fact is that we're all going to go through struggles in life, but God always brings us through them: Many are the afflictions of the righteous, but the Lord delivers us from *all* of them (Psalm 34:19). Never entertain a view of God that says He does not stand by us through our struggles.

As our Father, God has a character that maintains an irrevocable love, which will always act as a shield, protecting us from the difficulties of life. As with any shield, in order for us to receive God's safeguard, we must be in proper position to be protected. In other words, we must ensure that we are abiding by His will for our lives, not our own.

Certainly, we cannot confuse God's loving-kindness with weakness. God is the Judge of everything in the earth. God gives the ultimate verdict in each case of our lives. When God executes

His ruling, He uses His loving-kindness to make fair decisions. We can come to understand God by being well acquainted with His judgments.

My relationship with my mother is what helped me to live by God's judgments. When I was a young tyke, I remember asking my mother if I could go outside to play with a friend of mine. "Absolutely not. The last time you two played together, you got in trouble with the neighbors..." she said. A few weeks later, that same friend invited me to come play in his yard with him.

"Umm, my Mom isn't going to let me come outside to play with you," I said.

"How do you know when you haven't even asked her?" he wanted to know.

I shook my head and answered, "I don't have to ask because I remember what she said the last time. I know my mommy."

This is an example of how we can come to understand God by knowing His judgments. When we know God, we can use our knowledge of His character to understand how He's going to react or what He will decide in a situation before we even ask Him.

God is a perfect judge because He views everything through His righteous eyes. God's righteousness is the part of His character that makes Him impartial, honorable, and truthful. As a loving judge, God acts entirely on principles that are just and fair. In Jeremiah 9:24, the original Hebrew term for righteousness expresses that God is *sovereign in government*. His laws are the basis for all existence. As He speaks, He passes laws, and He only passes them in a loving manner.

Through His righteousness, we can be assured that no decision ever made by God has ever affected our lives in an unjust way. Ponder the circumstances of your life that you may classify as unloving treatment from God. You may have felt God was unfair because of certain circumstances you were forced to endure.

The solution to this is to understand what it means to describe the Lord as righteous—He can do no wrong. Knowing the righteousness of God's character helps us to understand that it is not God who is wrong. Instead, we must seek His understanding of the situation.

God, the Supreme Ruler, through His laws, creates everything on the earth as He sees fit. Each action of His will is righteous, holy, and sacred. When we faithfully serve Him, we declare His supremacy based on His most Holy Word. When we understand that God is righteous, we know that even if he makes a decision we absolutely loathe, His choice is the optimal solution for our lives.

God, our Holy Savior, takes delightful pleasure in all that is righteous. In every situation, God is going to do what is delightful to Him. What He does gives Him pleasure, and because He is the epitome of righteousness, whatever pleases Him will always be the correct choice to make. Since God delights in His decisions, we have no need to offer Him alternative solutions for our problems. Instead, if we choose to delight in the Lord, He will give us the desires of our heart (Psalm 37:4).

God's understanding concerning a situation will always match the correct understanding of Who He is. God will never break character. He is eternally consistent and makes no mistakes.

In all our ways we should acknowledge God so that He can direct our paths (Proverbs 3:6). As we become more aware of His character, we are less hasty to approach Him concerning certain matters that He has already addressed. Knowing God and obtaining His understanding of our lives is a sure way of acknowledging Him when our issues require His intervention.

Sometimes *knowing* what the understanding is equates only to our thoughts of what God says, but that is not a full representation of our hearts *getting* the understanding for any matter. We are comforted and encouraged by knowing what God's understanding is as we face hardships in our lives, but when the pressure of a life event becomes too hard for us to bear, it seems as if what we have learned struggles to surface in order to resolve the situation. In many occurrences, the understanding doesn't surface at all. Then a question arises in our souls, "Did we really *get* the understanding?"

CHAPTER 4
GETTING UNDERSTANDING

I began the difficult but rewarding adventure of playing the violin in the seventh grade. One of the first explanations we had was that the violin was among the most difficult instruments to learn because it provided no cue to the performer for playing the correct note.

Pianos have keys. Trumpets have valves. Drum sets have skins, symbols, and other pre-tuned parts, but the violin has no such attachments to aid in producing precise musical notes. The violinist has to believe that when he places his finger on a certain spot on the string, pressing it firmly on the fingerboard, that the correct note will be the result.

The teacher told the class that once we understood how to play the instrument, we would be an elite group of musicians because of our acquired skill, and she was right. As a teenager, I charged $20 per minute to play violin solos for certain events and had no problem being hired. Most of my clients wanted me to perform three-minute pieces of music for their functions.

I admit that the process of understanding how to play the violin was extremely challenging. I had to believe my teacher, Mrs. Thomason, when she told me that the notes I was playing were either too flat or too sharp. To top it all off, she had the God-given gift of perfect pitch, the ability to hear any note and recognize it without requiring any other resource for confirmation.

We had to put full faith in our instructor's lessons as being truth, or else we would never have understood how to effectively play our beautiful-sounding instruments. If we don't believe, we will never understand. For every single item that we want to understand, we have to believe the one who is giving the understanding, and of course, believe that the information being given is accurate.

Belief is crucial. Understanding can only be realized through belief. As citizens in the Kingdom of God (having received Jesus as Savior, Lord, and King, and faithfully serving), we obtain understanding by believing in God's Word.

Remembering that Scripture urges us to not lean to our own understanding, another facet of truth comes to light. Because our human minds are frail and clueless as to the future, leaning to our own understanding will prove to be inadequate when we're required to make important decisions. Having a firm foundation that we can draw on in difficult situations is vital to our making good choices for our lives and the lives of others.

The rough waves of circumstance are so intimidating at times that they cause us to doubt or even forget the understanding God has given to us. If we find that we have trouble seeing our lives the way God does, we need to perform a self-evaluation to analyze if we really did seek God sincerely in the first place. After all, during both calm and tumultuous times, we need to be able to recall and apply God's understanding at will.

One of the reasons why we don't get God's understanding during a crisis is because of the huge value, trust, and dependence we've placed on our own thoughts. When we completely remove our own ideas concerning an ordeal, only then can we fully accept the understanding God gives.

At one time, I faced a personal financial deficit. According to what I understood, I told God, "I need money." His response was unexpected. He said, "My son, you don't need money. Money needs you."

That was one of the greatest revelations concerning money I'd ever received. After hearing God's response, I changed my prayer to, "Father, give me understanding so that I will know what to do with money."

The only way to get *understanding* is to *trust* God 100 percent, with no wavering. These two italicized words are interchangeable. We could say, "I understand now that God is taking care of me" or "I trust now that God is taking care of me."

People come to me often about a situation they're facing, hoping that God will give me an answer for them. The first response I like to give is to ask, "What did God say to *you* when *you* prayed?" They may reply something like, "I've been praying and praying and praying, and God hasn't spoken to me yet!"

As a pastor, I know that my relationship with God is very respected by the congregants. I've always told them to go to God for themselves, and if they can't hear what God is saying, then come to me, and then I'll help them. I don't intend to be cruel or harsh, but I know that God wants a relationship with each of His children, and I'll *never* stand in the way of that relationship being built.

When we pray, we're tempted to pray according to what we see, and that can greatly hinder and even stop us from receiving God's Word. Therefore, we need to seek God's understanding of *every* position we find ourselves in, in life, so that we pray according to how *He* wants us to proceed.

Asking God for His Word when we find ourselves in a conundrum opens our hearts to receive His answer. Once we receive the answer, we can then pray in harmony with what He already wants to do. Praying for what God desires, versus what we desire, will insure every request will be fulfilled in agreement with God's purpose.

No matter how circumstances may appear, even if God isn't saying anything to you at the moment, still trust in Him. Understand that He *is* your Father, and He loves you. Whether He deems it necessary to speak to you about your problem or not, He always knows and provides what's best for His own. Trust Him.

Peter was one of Jesus' disciples. In the Bible, Peter is pointed to as walking on the water. And Peter did so because he asked that Jesus command him to, and thus, Jesus told Peter to come to Him. But Peter became frightened and began to sink. Later, Jesus asked Peter, "Why did you doubt?" (Matthew 14:28-31)

The original language that the New Testament was written in is Greek, and the interpretation for the Greek word *doubt* is *hesitation*.

When we don't fully trust, we will hesitate. Why do we hesitate after God has given us *His* Word? A lack of understanding is the culprit. Jesus said to Peter, "Come. ..." If Peter understood that the same command from Jesus to "Come..." also included the power on which his trust could walk securely, he wouldn't have sunk.

Trusting God causes us to act. Doubting God causes us to hesitate. If we stagger when we walk, we will stagger in the fulfillment of our destiny, in achieving our success.

It's time for us to hear God and trust Him wholeheartedly. We need to walk without hesitating, forgetting that the water is there. If the problem is our focus, doubting our success becomes easier than believing in it. If our focus is on God, He can always cause us to remember that walking on the water of our difficulties is not impossible once He commands us to do it.

> *There is a way which seemeth right unto a man, but the end thereof are the ways of death.*
>
> Proverbs 14:12 & 16:25, KJV

Trusting God is the *only* way to ultimate success in anyone's life. When we *don't* trust Him, we travel a road that will lead to our destruction, sooner or later.

Let's focus on a portion of the theme scripture, Proverbs 4:7 that states, "...*get Wisdom ... And with all you have gotten, get understanding....*"

The word *get* is placed before *wisdom* and *understanding* in the above scripture. A term originally from the Hebrew, it means to *acquire for oneself.* Get not only commands the reader to act, but its position here sheds light on the extreme importance of obtaining wisdom and understanding.

Since the responsibility has been firmly placed on the reader to obtain wisdom and understanding, how are these qualities to be acquired? Concerning wisdom, the Word of God declares the following:

> *If any of you is deficient in wisdom, let him ask of the giving God [Who gives] to everyone liberally and ungrudgingly, without*

reproaching or faultfinding, and it will be given him.

James 1:5

According to this scripture, getting wisdom requires three steps, and receiving it is as easy as standing in the ocean and letting the waves fall over you.

First, know that wisdom is a need.
Second, ask God for wisdom.
Lastly, have faith that God will grant it.

Obtaining understanding is a little more adventurous than gaining wisdom. Take a closer look at "...*with all you have gotten*...." Remember that the Hebrew definition for *get* is *to acquire for oneself.* The Hebrew definition for the word *gotten*, in this scripture, is *acquired by purchase.*

The definition of *gotten* is very significant because all of your current possessions were purchased. If they weren't purchased by you, they *were* purchased by someone else. Whether they were purchased using cash, time, or another currency, a cost was involved to acquire the items.

Think of a particular item that you have. What understanding did you get concerning the item? Did you perhaps read the owner's manual, or similar instructions?

However you received your understanding, I guarantee that certain information about your purchase was simply given to you, and you believed it. (Again, belief is a very important factor when getting understanding.) That belief convinced you to operate the item with full confidence, and it worked.

How do we receive understanding? We receive it by believing the information given to us. It's really that simple, but not always that easy to complete.

Information given may be as straightforward as, "If you clean out the refrigerator, that awful odor will vanish." Such information is received and believed. The instructions given are simple to understand, but implementing the understanding will take effort.

No matter how you slice it, the process of getting understanding requires our dedicated involvement. One of my favorite television shows is *Undercover Boss*. The program features top executives disguising themselves as entry-level workers.

The goal of these CEOs is to engage in first-hand interactions with employees and customers concerning the day-to-day operations of the companies and the experiences of the workers carrying out their jobs. At the end of each episode, the executives always reminisce, expressing the feeling that they leave their undercover venture with a greater understanding about the needs of their employees, customers, and their corporation.

On the show, the executives become emotional at times and show real humility at discovering their limitations and failings. They often reveal that their time with the front-line employees allowed them to see how out of touch they really were with the localized businesses in their corporation.

This show and the repeated findings of the bosses who go undercover points to the reality that if we believe we don't need input from another person because of our positions, we'll, indeed, fail to gain understanding. When others contribute advice based on their own experiences, that information offers understanding that will grow and could even save our enterprise, whatever that may be.

Being that my responsibility does not encompass everything in life, I'm not required to gain the understanding of all things. In my previous book, *What Are You Doing After the Dance?*, I shared that responsibility *is* your response to your ability.

"Do you understand everything, Dr. Wall?" someone may ask. I would respond by saying that I do not. I could easily point out that nobody understands everything, but I prefer to answer this way: I don't understand everything because I'm not responsible for everything.

Hundreds of students, faculty, and staff at Claflin University in Orangeburg, SC need to be fed meals daily. Because my father has the experience to properly prepare meals for such a number of people at one time, he was hired to use his ability to respond to that need. While my father is an expert in the kitchen, I rarely even cook. As a pastor, I am responsible for understanding how to befriend, encourage, and counsel people. I'm not required to understand what my position doesn't need.

Because we don't have the ability to do everything, we don't have to understand everything, but I do recommend that you understand everything you can about the abilities you possess so that you can cultivate them. That is your responsibility.

Everyone we hope to affect in life needs us to be at our very best. This is why as individuals we need to obtain the greatest level of understanding available to us about our own life's purpose.

CHAPTER 5
YOUR UNDERSTANDING

About 15 years ago, I seemed to develop a skill to manage Gospel recording artists. I managed Bishop Ronald E. Brown and Bryan Wilson. Both of these artists had a strong, unique following.

I was in charge of creating contracts to send to the promoters of the artists' concerts. Once a promoter signed the contract and submitted half of the performance fee, I would contact the band members, airline, bus and hotel companies to organize our trip.

I was also in charge of collecting the final payment in person from the promoters in addition to several other duties assisting in the promotion and management of these artists. God favored me, and I never accepted a bad deal in which my artists' funds came up short. I was also favored to receive many compliments from the artists, band members, and promoters. We ministered to thousands upon thousands of people domestically and internationally.

Several people urged me to open an artist management business because, in their estimation, I was a natural at it. I didn't consider myself to be a natural, however. My strategy was to research online and to ask questions of those I deemed to be the best in the business. In that way I was educated to understand what I needed to do.

Education is simply a sharing of understanding between one person and another. Nobody understands everything, but everybody understands at least one thing very well. For the most part, what we understand is the profession we desire to pursue. We follow our interests to become better educated about that area. Whatever you understand well, I encourage you to exercise, train, and rehearse your skills to support your unique ability.

Education provides positions of success that coincide with the degree of knowledge we have about a particular topic. The understanding we have attracts success. Once we understand, our level of understanding draws the appropriate success to it. The understanding of many influential individuals magnetizes a high degree of achievement.

For example, Michael Jordan, a six-time NBA champion and Hall-of-Famer, is successful because he understands the art of playing basketball. He has been hailed by many as the greatest to ever play the game. When he speaks about basketball, the sports world stops everything to listen. Likewise, Bill Gates, the co-founder of Microsoft, the world's largest software firm, would not have become the chairman and chief executive of his company if he'd lacked a solid understanding of computer technology. The same could be said for Tiger Woods, who is arguably the best professional golfer in the world. His superb understanding of golf led him to win fourteen major championships.

Some people may feel that their contributions to society are minuscule compared to another person's efforts. But instead of copying someone else's unique ability, we're taught in the Bible that we should increase in our own understanding to acquire our own skills.

In a world of copycats, don't you think it's time to introduce yourself to yourself by discovering your notable abilities that God has given you to understand? Don't waste your time trying to copy someone else's area of success. Everyone can have an understanding of an area that can bring great triumph. What is *your* understanding?

> *The wise also will hear and increase in learning, and the person of understanding will acquire skill and attain to sound counsel [so that he may be able to steer his course rightly]*
>
> Proverbs 1:5

No matter what your skill, it should be developed to the point where you should be the person others choose to go to in your area of expertise. In the Bible, King Solomon was building his house, and he needed someone to do some bronze work for him. A man named Hiram was known for his work with bronze, and so King Solomon sent a special request for him to come do the bronze work.

> *He was the son of a widow of the tribe of Naphtali, and his father was a man of Tyre, a worker in bronze. He was full of wisdom, understanding, and skill to do any kind of work in bronze. So he came to King Solomon and did all his [bronze] work.*
>
> 1 Kings 7:14

Hiram had the skill and understanding, so he was the only one who did the bronze work for the king. What understanding do you have that makes you the go-to person for your area of expertise? Think about yourself and your abilities. What is *your* understanding?

What knowledge do you have that would prompt the mayor, senators, or even the president to call on you for your expertise? What understanding do you have?

Understanding always gives birth to some kind of skill. But although a great amount of skill and understanding are important, they're not as critical as having the right attitude and wisdom. In order to be well suited for the work that we're called to do, we must be enthusiastic about undertaking the task.

> *Bezalel and Aholiab and every wisehearted man in whom the Lord has put wisdom and understanding to know how to do all the work for the service of the sanctuary shall work according to all that the Lord has commanded.*
>
> *And Moses called Bezalel and Aholiab and every able and wisehearted man in whose mind the Lord had put wisdom and ability, everyone whose heart stirred him up to come to do the work*
>
> Exodus 36:1-2

We can have the skill and talent, but few will put up with a terrible attitude. People would rather deal with someone who isn't as talented but has a great heart attitude, than someone who has excellent, skillful understanding, but poor people skills.

When we have the understanding of how to do something, God will put us in a position to work at what we understand. Instead of asking God for a job, ask God for an understanding that will get you a job, and an understanding of how to keep the job, as a bonus. Success is attracted to understanding, so when we ask God for understanding, we will find ourselves to be the favored ones for the position.

After we get the understanding, the right heart attitude, and the position, we'll want to use what God has given to us to our maximum abilities.

> *Whatever your hand finds to do, do it with all your might, for there is no work or device or knowledge or wisdom in Sheol (the place of the dead), where you are going.*
>
> Ecclesiastes 9:10

After we die, we will find no knowledge to be gained, wisdom to observe, or work to be completed. Everything, therefore, should be done to the best of our ability while we are on this earth. All that God has assigned us to do has to be done before we die. Even as we use our understanding to be of service, we must seek God to know what He wants us to do, realizing that it's important to do only what God desires in our lives.

> *I returned and saw under the sun that the race is not to the swift nor the battle to the strong, neither is bread to the wise nor riches to men of intelligence and understanding nor*

> *favor to men of skill; but time and chance
> happen to them all.*
>
> Ecclesiastes 9:11

In reference to *time* and *chance*, the original language of the Old Testament records that *uncertainty* and *occurrences* happen to everyone. If we stick to trying to do the will of God through difficult seasons, we'll have nothing to fear while navigating through the shadow of death (Psalm 23:4). If we don't do the will of God, these uncertain and negative occurrences can destroy everything that God has given to us. This makes staying under His wing while following the path He directs important, lest we stray into a place not indicated by His understanding.

The enemy's plan is to distract us from fulfilling God's purpose in our lives. By leading us down a path of sin, the devil wants to pervert God's understanding and to hinder the Lord's plans from being fulfilled. We need to surround ourselves with those who are being led in the right direction and who will help us bring our lives into full achievement, as the Father desires.

We must be careful of who we're following. We will arrive at the same destination as those we follow. Don't be led by those who are lazy, slack, unstable, and undisciplined. If we don't have someone in our lives who has a greater understanding than we do, where are we going? Show me your friends, and I will show you your future.

I admit that I need people around me who know more than I do so that I can grow and advance. For you to accomplish this as well, I encourage you to be free from a routine that hasn't greatly profited you. Go meet some people who will take you higher in wisdom and understanding and then apply what you learn to your life.

During the process of sharpening your skills, you'll encounter those who'll need your specific ability. Feel free to enjoy the rewards of someone coming to you for understanding. You'll deserve the positive attention due to all your hard work. However, if you happen to come across someone who desires your understanding about a matter you have yet to master, you should know how to relate to that person as well. In other words, your understanding should be mature enough for you to relate to someone whether or not you have prior experience in that specific area of need.

CHAPTER 6

UNDERSTANDING BEYOND EXPERIENCE

As believers, we have the responsibility to serve one another. To that end, God has given us the ability to transcend the limited capacity of our own experiences. We can minister to each other even without going through the same difficulties. The Word of God has given us the following command in the book of Romans.

> *Live in harmony with one another; do not be haughty (snobbish, high-minded, exclusive), but readily adjust yourself to [people, things] and give yourselves to humble tasks. Never overestimate yourself or be wise in your own conceits.*

> Romans 12:16

In helping each other, we must humble ourselves and seek to counsel each other whether or not we've faced the same difficulties as our brothers and sisters in the Lord.

I have the pleasure of pastoring a local church here in Orangeburg, SC. In all my years of pastoring, I've been approached countless times by members for consolation. When congregants first began to look to me for comfort, I often found myself astounded by the fact that I was easily able to console them without having gone through what they had experienced.

In one particular instance, I was trying to provide solace to a woman who had decided to avoid going to church because of the death of her three toddlers. She came to me weeping, her face contorted, yearning to have her precious babies back in her arms. I listened to her bawling outcries of despair, knowing I could provide her with little help other than prayer. One after the other, tears streamed down her face. Her sobs were loud, yet so meek in desperation. All she wanted was to see her children again. She knew I could do nothing, but she longed to talk to someone who would hear what she was going through. She wanted someone who could understand. I wanted to be that person.

I tried to support her the way anyone else would who hadn't come face to face with such traumatic, life-altering events. Patting her on the back, I said the only empathetic words I could think of: "I understand."

I've never had a child who died. Actually, I've never had any children at all. I was completely out of touch with what she was going through. Nevertheless, I genuinely wanted her to know that I could relate to her pain. I wanted her to know she wasn't alone. After my response, she looked up at me, her eyes angrily piercing in my direction. Her eyebrows furrowed, and her face tightened as she narrowed each eyelid, as if to look at me with only a small fraction of her sight.

She yelled in fury, "How dare you say you *understand*?! You've never gone through this before! How can you say that you understand what I'm going through?!"

I was taken aback. I thought that I was being compassionate, telling her what I knew would reassure her. What could my response be? That I was sorry? Or that I didn't mean it? My intention was never to be insensitive. Since all my words were sincere, I didn't feel as if I needed to apologize. I didn't know what I should do. I was baffled.

Instead of apologizing, I said the only words I knew: "I understand everything you went through because I *believe* you."

I continued, "I believe every wailing cry, every bitter tear, every painful memory, and every aching heartbeat. I haven't gone through what you have, but I *believe* with every bit of my being that what you have told me is true."

I needed her to know she was being cared for by me. I wanted her to realize that God desired to call her to a place of comfort and peace. Fortunately, she accepted my explanation and grasped my expression of the only way I knew to possibly relate to her without my having had a similar experience.

I thank God that I was able to explain to the woman who had lost her children that we don't have to be exposed to situations, events, or encounters to relate to them. All we simply need to do is *believe* what we are being told.

For example, the Bible contains many life circumstances that I have yet to undergo. Unlike Jonah, I have never had the torment of being trapped alive in the belly of a whale for three days. However, because I believe with faith that the story is true, I can understand that God uses Jonah's situation to teach me the importance of obedience.

When it comes to the guarantees that are given to us as Kingdom citizens, many of us imagine that we need to have experienced what the Bible promises *before* we can believe what the Bible teaches. However, needing to have an experience before *believing* is the complete opposite of walking by faith.

We have no way to understand anything in Scripture if we don't believe. Our level of understanding is literally equal to our level of belief. Experience is not a prerequisite for understanding. The only prerequisite is faith.

Now that we're aware that believing can cause us to understand without having experienced certain situations, our belief in God must subscribe to the same attitude of faith.

We have no way to believe in what God says if we don't get to know Him first. Some people become better acquainted with their situations than with God Himself. We must have faith in what God is saying to us, and His character is what makes Him truly believable. We know that God cannot lie. Therefore, we believe everything that He says. Paul's letter to Timothy illustrates the principle that intimacy with God births belief in Him.

> *And this is why I am suffering as I do. Still I am not ashamed, for I know (perceive, have knowledge of, and am acquainted with) Him Whom I have believed (adhered to and trusted in and relied on)...*
>
> 2 Timothy 1:12a

In other words, in order to believe, we must have a strong stance in our minds that affirms God's character.

If you doubt God, you really don't know Him— personally. Who is God to you?

The more you know Him, the more your faith and trust in Him develops.

How much time did you spend in prayer yesterday? By the way, when I say prayer, I mean conversation. There's no way you can get to know anyone if the conversation is one sided. Let God speak in prayer and *believe* what He says.

While it's important to trust our brothers' and sisters' abilities to understand our situations despite their not having experienced them, we must be sure that the brother or sister we are receiving advice from is only hearing from the Lord, not their own thoughts. When we refuse to believe God's understanding, we tend to go elsewhere to receive clarity.

The problem is that any source contrary to the Word of God will always lead us astray. People who are weak in their faith tend to go to other like-minded individuals for pity.

A church member who is unfaithful in her church attendance will probably go to someone else who is equally unreliable in the same area, who says, "I don't see why going to every service is such a big deal." Unfortunately, that church member will miss a valuable Word from the Lord because of the person she has chosen to believe.

As we abide in the Lord, we must treat our lives as if disobedience or disbelief is not an option. He owns our lives, but if we rebel, He will still deliver His Word to the others who are attentive to what He provides.

When we enter into salvation, God's rules become the rules by which we live. Our way of life has to be to adhere to God, only following His plans. Anything else is detrimental to both our lives and our relationship with the Lord.

When people believe what others tell them in error, they'll act according to that misaligned understanding. When we are guided by misconceptions, our lives begin to reflect that something is incorrect about the information we're receiving.

Blinded by our own perceptions of truth, we go through life praying and hoping for God to meet us somewhere He hasn't promised. Subsequently, we miss the opportunity to be where God has told us He would be.

The truth is that God's purpose for our lives will always be greater than our own. While we can only know a fraction of what He has prepared for us, His foresight goes much further.

We can't always see what He has ordained, but we can understand through belief that God has prepared special lives for us. When we accede to God's understanding, our actions will be filled with faith and love.

If we refuse to believe that God's ways are better than ours, we will wrongly try to force our own understanding into a life that He already owns. Consequently, we become frustrated and impatient because what we *thought* we wanted comes with the havoc that God was trying to protect us from.

The way to avoid unnecessary troubles is to simply believe God's understanding of every life situation and to know that His will is always superior to our own. If we can trust God, our daily actions will directly correlate with our obedience. We will be clear about where we are headed with the Lord.

A key to walking in tune with God's will is knowing and believing in His identity. We have been graced with the Old Testament writings of the Prophet Isaiah who proclaimed Who God truly is.

> *You are My witnesses, says the Lord, and My*
> *servant whom I have chosen, that you may*
> *know Me, believe Me and remain steadfast*
> *to Me, and understand that I am He. Before*

Me there was no God formed, neither shall there be after Me.

Isaiah 43:10

God commands His people through Isaiah to understand that He is the all-powerful, parentless, Creator. The Lord wants us to know that He is not limited by mortal strength or miniscule imagination.

God knows that we must first *believe* in Who He is in order to *understand* Who He is. As we sometimes see, many people who read the Word of God still say, "I just really don't understand walking by faith, or the working of miracles." The Bible readers who make such a claim can't understand because they refuse to believe in the greatness of God. They are in complete opposition to the Word of God.

If I am not doing the works [performing the deeds] of My Father, then do not believe Me [do not adhere to Me and trust Me and rely on Me]. But if I do them, even though you do not believe Me or have faith in Me, [at least] believe the works and have faith in what I do, in order that you may know and understand [clearly] that the Father is in Me, and I am in the Father [One with Him]

John 10:37-38

Understanding what God says while trying to retain our own beliefs is an impossibility. In order to understand, we must believe what He is saying or teaching. Such is the case in the following true life story.

A group of missionaries traveled all the way from the United States to South Africa to meet an evangelist who journeyed around the continent to find people who had died. The evangelist's ministry focused on raising people from the dead.

Ironically, although they were believers too, the missionaries were eager to see *how* the man was able to accomplish this feat. They had read the same Word of God that this man had, yet his actions left them astounded and confused. They didn't understand.

They followed the man from town to town, watching in amazement as corpse after corpse was raised from the dead. The man would go to a town or village, and he would roar, "Who died today?" The townspeople would lead the man to someone who had died. Pointing at the body, the man would pray in a strong, booming voice, "God, is this death from You, or is it from the devil?" If God told the man that the person's death was not His will, he would point his finger at the corpse and yell, "I command you to get up in the name of the Lord Jesus Christ."

Dumbfounded, the missionaries would watch in total astonishment as the body stirred and eventually raised up, completely revived.

"How can you do such things?" they asked.

The man shook his head.

"Don't you read your Bible?"

"Yes, we read the Bible, but—"

"Doesn't the Bible say that we can raise the dead? That we can do even greater works than Jesus did?"

"Yes, we've read that in the Bible, but we don't understand exactly how you do it."

The man was aghast at their lack of faith.

The missionaries tried to understand while bypassing belief. They didn't want to humble themselves by sacrificing the limitations that hindered them from understanding. They read the Bible, but because they didn't believe, their understanding of their capabilities was their own, not the Lord's.

When it's hard for you to understand something, often, it's simply because you don't believe it. The position of your belief is literally the limit of your understanding.

We need to understand *beyond* experience. We must believe in our abilities to achieve what God has said is possible before actually accomplishing the task. We need to see the success that He has promised us before actually crossing the finish line. This is what it means to walk by faith: As Christians, we don't always know the next step that lies ahead, but we rely on and trust the Lord to grant us victory in every trial.

Being victorious is an innate human desire that God has included in the hearts of each of us. Achievement is expected and attainable, but we should never scheme our way into becoming successful. Instead, we can access the keys to God's Kingdom, ways to operate in accord with God's majestic power here on earth, ways that Jesus Himself revealed thousands of years ago, and that are still discoverable and can be applied to our lives today.

CHAPTER 7
KINGDOM KEYS OF UNDERSTANDING

I was moved to tears. I said to God, "Lord, I'm sorry. I am so very sorry..."

I was hurt. I felt as if I wanted to console God—as if He needed any consolation—but I just knew that I had to do something. I had to tell people how God felt! I just had to let them know!

I was preparing to teach Bible study that evening. I had sent out a mass text telling the members that the message I was about to deliver had truly moved me.

I had come across a verse I'd never noticed before in all my years of studying the Bible:

> *Then all the elders of Israel gathered themselves together, and came to Samuel unto Ramah,*
>
> *And said unto him, Behold, thou art old, and thy sons walk not in thy ways: now make us a king to judge us like all the nations.*
>
> *But the thing displeased Samuel, when they said, Give us a king to judge us. And Samuel prayed unto the LORD.*

> *And the LORD said unto Samuel, Hearken*
> *unto the voice of the people in all that they*
> *say unto thee: for they have not rejected thee,*
> *but they have rejected me, that I should not*
> *reign over them.*
>
> 1 Samuel 8:4-7, KJV

The Israelites, God's people in the Bible, were ruled by the Lord and His prophets. Samuel, a prophet who faithfully served God from his youth, was confronted by the elders of Israel because they wanted a king to rule over them. Then, I read what the Prophet Samuel said in response to the elders. This is the other verse that touched my heart so deeply, moving me to tears:

> *And when ye saw that Nahash the king of*
> *the children of Ammon came against you,*
> *ye said unto me, Nay; but a king shall reign*
> *over us: when the LORD your God was your*
> *king.*
>
> 1 Samuel 12:12, KJV

The children of Israel wanted to be like Ammon and the idol worshipping nations that had kings ruling over them. By seeking a king, the people had rejected God, Who created, loved, and protected them. They literally dethroned God as king just so they could be like everyone else.

How could anyone reject the Almighty God as being their king? Immediately after reading that the elders of Israel told Samuel they didn't not want God as their king, I repented. I thought about the times that I didn't honor God as *my* king.

I heard preachers and other Christians mention the *Kingdom of God*. I understood the term as just another way fellow Christians communicated to each other how blessed we are to be a part of God's church worldwide. I never really thought any deeper about what that term meant.

I have heard powerful sermons by Dr. Myles Munroe, a pastor from Nassau, Bahamas, who has written best-selling books on the Kingdom of God. His sermons prompted me to conduct a personal Bible study on the subject for over a year.

One of the scriptures I studied relates how Jesus asked His disciples what the word around town was concerning His identity:

> *When Jesus came into the coasts of Caesarea Philippi, he asked his disciples, saying, Whom do men say that I the Son of man am?*
>
> *And they said, Some say that thou art John the Baptist: some, Elias; and others, Jeremias, or one of the prophets.*
>
> *He saith unto them, But whom say ye that I am?*
>
> *And Simon Peter answered and said, Thou art the Christ, the Son of the living God.*
>
> *And Jesus answered and said unto him, Blessed art thou, Simon Barjona: for flesh and blood hath not revealed it unto thee, but my Father which is in Heaven.*
>
> Matthew 16:13-17, KJV

God revealed to Peter, one of Jesus' closest disciples, something that many people were unsure of. Our heavenly Father showed Peter that Jesus was His Son. After Jesus gave Peter an opportunity to share his revelation, our Lord made a remarkable promise to him.

> *And I say also unto thee, That thou art Peter, and upon this rock I will build my church; and the gates of hell shall not prevail against it.*
> *And I will give unto thee the keys of the kingdom of Heaven: and whatsoever thou shalt bind on earth shall be bound in Heaven: and whatsoever thou shalt loose on earth shall be loosed in Heaven.*
> Matthew 16:18-19, KJV

Jesus gave Peter the keys to the Kingdom of Heaven. Can you imagine receiving these keys from Jesus Christ Himself?

It seemed as if Jesus was impressed by Peter's sensitivity to God, the One Who revealed to Peter Who Jesus actually was. Therefore, Jesus explained to Peter that the keys He would give him would empower him to bind and loose on the earth, but there was a prerequisite to using that power.

The term *bind* refers to declaring what is considered illegal. The term *loose* refers to declaring what is considered legal. We can replace the words *bind* and *loose* in the reference scripture with the terms *illegal* and *legal*, respectively. Thus, the verse above can be paraphrased as "*Whatever you make legal on earth, must be what is already legal in Heaven. Whatever you make illegal on earth, must be what is already illegal in Heaven.*"

For example, there's no sickness in Heaven because it cannot legally operate there, and that law is strictly enforced. With the possession of the Kingdom keys, we have the authority to forbid sickness to function in our lives because of its illegal status. When we know for ourselves Who Jesus is and obtain the keys to the Kingdom, we can successfully enforce and apply the laws of Heaven to our everyday earthly situations.

Many scriptural references confirm Who Jesus is and how we can enjoy a bountiful relationship with Him, but I didn't know the whereabouts of the biblical record that disclosed the eventful transfer of the keys from Jesus to Peter. I pondered on how awesome it would be for people to have those keys right *now*, especially amid the crises we all face during this day and time. My thoughts were that maybe if that moment was included in the Bible, I could somehow recreate such a moment to receive the keys myself.

I searched the Bible to know where the keys were, but I couldn't find the incidents where Jesus literally transferred the keys to Peter. Then the Holy Spirit guided me to an epiphany. To find the keys of the Kingdom, the Holy Spirit said to me, "From the point where Jesus promised the keys of the Kingdom to Peter, find each time where Jesus said something that directly related to Peter. At each of those points, you will find a key to the Kingdom."

The Holy Spirit guided me to discover those moments in scripture and I found the keys. The keys of the Kingdom are inclusive of acts of obedience, and they also open wide the door to God's favor and miracles in our lives.

When the term *key* is used metaphorically it refers to how to understand a specific subject matter. For example, some may say the *key* to studying science is to take great notes. Others may say the *key* to playing an instrument well is to practice daily. The purpose of the *keys* to Heaven are no different. Through the Kingdom keys, we can establish a firm understanding of the Kingdom of God.

It is now my pleasure to present to you what the Holy Spirit uncovered for me. This chapter's length exceeds the others in this book, but I would be remiss if I withheld or even drastically abridged this section, as it is the crux of understanding God's Kingdom, making the power of the Kingdom available to us.

Key #1: Savor the things that be of God.

> *From that time forth began Jesus to shew unto his disciples, how that he must go unto Jerusalem, and suffer many things of the elders and chief priests and scribes, and be killed, and be raised again the third day.*
>
> *Then Peter took him, and began to rebuke him, saying, Be it far from thee, Lord: this shall not be unto thee.*
>
> *But he turned, and said unto Peter, Get thee behind me, Satan: thou art an offence unto me: for thou savourest not the things that be of God, but those that be of men.*
>
> Matthew 16:21-23, KJV

To savor means to be intent—concentrated, focused, fixed—on promoting only what God wills. Jesus knew that God's will was for Him to die and be raised from the dead. But Peter relished his relationship with Jesus, so much so that he wanted Jesus to avoid God's purpose for His life, martyrdom. Peter didn't savor the things of God and Jesus sharply rebuked him.

Key #2: Don't fear—hear.

> *And after six days Jesus taketh with him Peter, and James, and John, and leadeth them up into an high mountain apart by themselves: and he was transfigured before them.*
>
> *And his raiment became shining, exceeding white as snow; so as no fuller on earth can white them.*
>
> *And there appeared unto them Elias with Moses: and they were talking with Jesus.*
>
> *And Peter answered and said to Jesus, Master, it is good for us to be here: and let us make three tabernacles; one for thee, and one for Moses, and one for Elias.*
>
> *For he wist not what to say; for they were sore afraid.*
>
> *And there was a cloud that overshadowed them: and a voice came out of the cloud, saying, This is my beloved Son: hear him.*
>
> Mark 9:2-7, KJV

Jesus took his closest disciples, Peter, James, and John to a mountain where He was transfigured into a supernatural form. When the Old Testament figures Moses and Elijah appeared with Jesus during His transfiguration, Peter became frightened. Then

God spoke audibly from Heaven and declared that Jesus was His Son, and He instructed the disciples to hear Jesus, meaning to intently listen to whatever Jesus said to them.

What happens when we start fearing? We immediately want to jump into action. Who in Heaven is fearing?

The mother of one of my spiritual sons called me on the phone, speaking in a panicked voice.

"Are you back there with Clifton?" she asked.

"No, ma'am, I'm not. How are you doing today?" I responded, while leaning against a bedroom doorway.

"Clifton has been in an accident. His car flipped four times, and he's in critical condition at the hospital. I thought you were in the room with him."

My heart started to race as I began to pray immediately under my breath while his mother continued to talk. My immediate instinct was to allow the present fear to grip me, to dive into despair. But the key is to hear, not fear. I stood up a little straighter and concentrated on what God was telling me rather than on what the young man's mother was saying. I heard the Holy Spirit speak clearly in my ear: "He is not going to die."

After hearing God's declaration from Heaven, I spoke directly to the devil.

"Clifton is not going to die, you foul force! I rebuke you in the name of Jesus. You cannot take his life! I don't know everything that happened on the scene of the accident, but I do know that Clifton is *not* going to die!"

What was sent from Heaven was declared on earth, and it came to pass. I arrived at the hospital a couple of hours later and found Clifton in critical condition. I laid hands on him and prayed for him. God gave him a remarkable recovery, and he is alive today with absolutely no complications from the accident.

Key #3: Think who you are.

> *And when they were come to Capernaum, they that received tribute money came to Peter, and said, Doth not your master pay tribute?*
>
> *He saith, Yes. And when he was come into the house, Jesus prevented him, saying, What thinkest thou, Simon? of whom do the kings of the earth take custom or tribute? of their own children, or of strangers?*
>
> *Peter saith unto him, Of strangers. Jesus saith unto him, Then are the children free.*
>
> *Notwithstanding, lest we should offend them, go thou to the sea, and cast an hook, and take up the fish that first cometh up; and when thou hast opened his mouth, thou shalt find a piece of money: that take, and give unto them for me and thee.*
>
> Matthew 17:24-27, KJV

Tax collectors approached Peter and asked if Jesus paid taxes. Peter said, "Yes." When he arrived where Jesus was, the first point that Jesus made to him was the fact that Peter wasn't thinking properly. According to the Kingdom mentality, Peter was thinking an illegal thought.

When we think who we are, we won't make as many mistakes because we're constantly thinking about our integrity, living a life that pleases God and represents Jesus well. If we settle for just passively *knowing* who we are, we'll still fall short of pleasing God because we aren't constantly thinking about the Godly characteristics we're responsible for displaying.

Key #4: Unforgiveness is illegal for you and everyone else.

> *Then came Peter to him, and said, Lord, how oft shall my brother sin against me, and I forgive him? till seven times? Jesus saith unto him, I say not unto thee, Until seven times: but, Until seventy times seven.*
>
> Matthew 18:21-22, KJV

When Jesus said that we should forgive our fellow man seventy times seven times, He didn't mean 490 times. In the culture of Jesus' day, seventy times seven meant countless times. Even in the face of grave injustice, we must forgive.

Someone who lost a loved one may say, "I don't know if I'll ever be able to forgive him. He killed my son!"

But many times we confuse forgiveness and forgetting. Forgiveness is an old banking term used when the customer has made the last payment on her loan. When the loan was paid in full, the contract for the loan would be stamped FORGIVEN, and a copy would be given to the customer.

This same concept applies to relationships. When we have truly forgiven someone, we must release him from the debt of what we feel he owes us and make a personal announcement in our hearts concerning the offender by saying, "You owe me nothing, not even an apology." Forgiving a person doesn't prevent us from becoming wary of the individual who has harmed us, but it does release us from the weight of carrying anger, bitterness, and other hard feelings in our hearts toward our offenders.

Key #5: Whatever you have forsaken is sown for abundance.

> *Then answered Peter and said unto him, Behold, we have forsaken all, and followed thee; what shall we have therefore?*
>
> *And Jesus said unto them, Verily I say unto you, That ye which have followed me, in the regeneration when the Son of man shall sit in the throne of his glory, ye also shall sit upon twelve thrones, judging the twelve tribes of Israel.*
>
> *And every one that hath forsaken houses, or brethren, or sisters, or father, or mother, or wife, or children, or lands, for my name's sake, shall receive an hundredfold, and shall inherit everlasting life.*
>
> *But many that are first shall be last; and the last shall be first.*
>
> Matthew 19:27-30, KJV

Peter asked Jesus what he and the other disciples would receive as a reward for what they sacrificed to follow Him.

Everything you have abandoned for the sake of living for God, He considers to be seeds planted for abundance. Seeds are small—a tiny seed can turn into a flower, a bush, or even a large oak tree. As we sow seeds in God's Kingdom, we'll always reap the very best that God has to offer, because He's the One Who commands the ground that receives our seeds to grow whatever has been sowed in it. God's best is always better than anything we can ever imagine for ourselves.

Key #6: God knows us better than we know ourselves. We must believe His Word over our own.

> Then saith Jesus unto them, All ye shall be offended because of me this night: for it is written, I will smite the shepherd, and the sheep of the flock shall be scattered abroad.
>
> But after I am risen again, I will go before you into Galilee.
>
> Peter answered and said unto him, Though all men shall be offended because of thee, yet will I never be offended.
>
> Jesus said unto him, Verily I say unto thee, That this night, before the cock crow, thou shalt deny me thrice.
>
> Peter said unto him, Though I should die with thee, yet will I not deny thee. Likewise also said all the disciples.
>
> Matthew 26:31-35, KJV

Even though Peter said in this passage that he wouldn't deny Jesus, Peter denied Him three times, and the Bible declares to us that Peter even used profanity to try to prove that he wasn't associated with Christ. Jesus knew that Peter's denials would happen.

As a pastor, I often take notice when one of my members is lacking spiritually. After letting him know what he needs to improve, I'm often met with excuses. It's very easy to relieve ourselves of the responsibility of upholding God's expectations of us, but no excuse will be allowed when we're standing in front of Jesus Christ to account for our time on earth. Can you imagine someone trying to vindicate himself by saying, "I'm sorry, Jesus. I didn't witness to my friend because I didn't want her to think that I was weird."

Instead of coming up with a justification, we need to realize that God knows us and is calling us higher in His purpose. He has no need for excuses and disobedience. If the feat of witnessing wasn't possible to achieve, then God wouldn't assign it to us. He knows better than we do what we're capable of handling.

So, when the Creator of the Universe picks *you* to accomplish a task, trust His choice. Don't believe the lies of Satan that will tell you, "I can't do this. I'm not equipped to finish that." God knows us better than we know ourselves, and He wouldn't waste His time assigning duties to someone He thought couldn't complete them. If He has chosen you, all that is left to do is to trust and believe.

> *Fear not, little flock; for it is your Father's*
> *good pleasure to give you the kingdom.*
> *Be ye therefore ready also: for the Son of*
> *man cometh at an hour when ye think not.*
> Luke 12:32, 40, KJV

When Jesus comes back, it'll be at a time when we're not thinking about His return. This is important because we have to be living saved every second—not just every day—of our lives.

Key #7: Increase comes to the worker who is prepared for and faithfully does the will of the King.

> *Then Peter said unto him, Lord, speakest thou this parable unto us, or even to all?*
>
> *And the Lord said, Who then is that faithful and wise steward, whom his lord shall make ruler over his household, to give them their portion of meat in due season?*
>
> *Blessed is that servant, whom his lord when he cometh shall find so doing.*
>
> *Of a truth I say unto you, that he will make him ruler over all that he hath.*
>
> Luke 12:41-44, KJV

Jesus has left the earth, but when He returns, are you going to be caught working for His glory? Will you be carrying out the tasks that God has willed for your life? Will you be able to tell God how many people you helped get saved through your personal ministry? When God sees that we have been active in His will, He will bring increase to our lives.

What are we doing to fulfill God's purpose? The Bible says that no one knows the day nor the hour, but I would imagine that Jesus wouldn't return on a Sunday. I imagine it being on a random day and time, like maybe a Thursday at 5:34 p.m., a moment when we would least expect Jesus to return. This shouldn't be a problem if we're constantly thinking who we are.

> *Jesus knowing that the Father had given all things into his hands, and that he was come from God, and went to God;*
> *He riseth from supper, and laid aside his garments; and took a towel, and girded himself.*
> *After that he poureth water into a bason, and began to wash the disciples' feet, and to wipe them with the towel wherewith he was girded.*
> *Then cometh he to Simon Peter: and Peter saith unto him, Lord, dost thou wash my feet?*
>
> John 13:3-6, KJV

In Jesus' time, most people traveled on dirty, dusty roadways by foot, many of them wearing only sandals. When a guest arrived in a home, it was customary for the lowest-ranking slave to wash the guest's feet of all of the dirt and debris that had accumulated during travel. Jesus began to wash Peter's feet, but Peter wouldn't allow it because he knew that his Lord was no slave.

Key #8: God sends us to serve each other, and no service is too humbling.

Peter saith unto him, Thou shalt never wash my feet. Jesus answered him, If I wash thee not, thou hast no part with me.

Simon Peter saith unto him, Lord, not my feet only, but also my hands and my head.

Jesus saith to him, He that is washed needeth not save to wash his feet, but is clean every whit: and ye are clean, but not all.

For he knew who should betray him; therefore said he, Ye are not all clean.

So after he had washed their feet, and had taken his garments, and was set down again, he said unto them, Know ye what I have done to you?

Ye call me Master and Lord: and ye say well; for so I am.

If I then, your Lord and Master, have washed your feet; ye also ought to wash one another's feet.

For I have given you an example, that ye should do as I have done to you.

Verily, verily, I say unto you, The servant is not greater than his lord; neither he that is sent greater than he that sent him.

If ye know these things, happy are ye if ye do them.

John 13:8-17, KJV

Someone with a high paying job may say, "I make six figures. I'm not going to someone's house to sweep the floor just because her arthritis is flaring up."

We are sent by God to serve, and Jesus showed it by washing his disciples' feet. Instead of talking about what we're going to do to help, we have to put our helping hands into action. We hear this particular phrase frequently, often coming from our own mouths: "If you ever need anything, just let me know." What happens when that person calls requesting a big favor? Are we indignant, and do we feel annoyed at the prospect of someone calling us at our word, or do we jump into action with a serving and helpful heart?

Key #9: Actively do the will of God and pray. Only then will you not enter into temptation.

> *And he went a little farther, and fell on his face, and prayed, saying, O my Father, if it be possible, let this cup pass from me: nevertheless not as I will, but as thou wilt.*
>
> *And he cometh unto the disciples, and findeth them asleep, and saith unto Peter, What, could ye not watch with me one hour?*
>
> *Watch and pray, that ye enter not into temptation: the spirit indeed is willing, but the flesh is weak.*
>
> Matthew 26:39-41, KJV

Jesus asked God, His Father, if this cup could pass from Him—so that Jesus wouldn't have to go through the agony of the last days of His life. Even though Jesus knew exactly what would happen to Him, including the pain that He would endure, Jesus still wanted His Father's will to be done in His life.

Just because temptation is presented doesn't mean that we have to enter into it. Jesus had strict control over His life and it's important that we follow His example. Had He been loose with His life, Jesus would have listened to His flesh and avoided God's will for His life, which would seemingly be death.

Only if we are actively carrying out the Word of God and praying, will we not enter into temptation. If our minds are focused and stayed on God, we leave no room for evil thoughts or tempting lies from the enemy.

> *Ye are they which have continued with me in my temptations.*
>
> *And I appoint unto you a kingdom, as my Father hath appointed unto me;*
>
> *That ye may eat and drink at my table in my kingdom, and sit on thrones judging the twelve tribes of Israel.*
>
> *And the Lord said, Simon, Simon, behold, Satan hath desired to have you, that he may sift you as wheat*
>
> Luke 22:28-31, KJV

Jesus was telling Peter that the devil desired to have him, meaning devils literally ask God for people to be moved beyond His power so that they can test their faith with attacks of affliction. Jesus told Peter how He responded to the knowledge of the desired attacks, and He gave Peter instructions.

Key #10: Prayer keeps faith from failing so that we can provide strength to one another.

> *But I have prayed for thee, that thy faith fail not: and when thou art converted, strengthen thy brethren.*
>
> *And he said unto him, Lord, I am ready to go with thee, both into prison, and to death.*
>
> *And he said, I tell thee, Peter, the cock shall not crow this day, before that thou shalt thrice deny that thou knowest me.*
>
> Luke 22:32-34, KJV

Jesus is telling us that we have to pray to keep our faith strong, and if we fail to pray, our faith will become weak. We then won't be strong enough to build up our brothers and sisters.

Communication and communion with God is critical to our spiritual lives. The average Christian prays for less than ten minutes per day. We need to spend ample time with God each day so that we can learn His will and be strong for others. This means spending time daily in prayer. We should make it a habit to provide time during the day to spend with our heavenly Father. We can get to bed early so that we can get up early for prayer. Then, we must continue praying all throughout the day to keep that connection with God open.

Now that the keys of the Kingdom have been given to us, we are responsible for faithfully applying them to our daily lives by living according to the keys. We then are expected and empowered to declare the Godly legalities of situations regarding our lives and the lives of others who need to understand.

CHAPTER 8
THE ONE WHO UNDERSTANDS

We must never lean unto our own understanding, not even for a moment. Our limited ability to accurately judge circumstances should make us desperate to understand our lives the way God does. When the Lord teaches us how we should think, we must remain loyal to the knowledge that He has given us. If we align our understanding with people who don't know Jesus, we risk rejecting God's plans for our entire lives. If we listen to those who view life through the cloudy lenses of ungodliness, we will head toward horrific life changes. Their counsel can cause us to go from serving God to serving ourselves. One faulty influence can be enough to blind us entirely from the path of truth that God has set for us.

I once knew this young man, Kevin, whom I affectionately refer to as my spiritual son. He didn't have many positive influences. His parents were drug addicts living on the street. Nevertheless, Kevin conquered his surroundings through serving the Lord after being saved at the tender age of eight.

The Lord made Kevin appear quite mature and wise for his age. One day after worship service, he came to me, saying, "Pastor Wall, I finally understand my life. I might not have the parents I want, but I should be grateful that I have parents at all. I can bring my Mom, Dad, and the rest of my family to Christ. That's what the Lord has wanted all this time. I finally get it. I finally understand!"

I smiled pleasantly at the glowing realization beaming like a beacon of light off this little boy's face. Ever since he'd received salvation, it was apparent to everyone around him, including me, that this boy had a strong calling to be a preacher. He could quote scriptures and witness to people as if he were an adult with years of experience. What a profound blessing seeing the work of the Lord in this young servant of God.

Sadly, at about 16 years old, Kevin allowed peer pressure to cause his fall. Kevin's hunger to obey God subsided. He would make statements such as, "Why should I care about my life if my own parents don't even care about me?"

By 17, Kevin was on drugs and addicted to alcohol. He dropped out of school without any plans for the future. I was astounded to witness such an intense transformation.

As time passed, God's dire concern for Kevin's change of lifestyle heightened. The Holy Spirit gave me an unexpected vision along with a strong urgency to check up on the young man.

"Hello, son, how are you?"

"Hey, Dad. I'm okay, I guess." His response was hesitant, but then he continued, "What's up?" From the moment he'd picked up the phone, my concerned voice let him know that something was wrong.

"Son, I'm glad you answered the phone. The Holy Spirit showed me a startling vision of you getting struck by a car. Please rededicate your life to God. You've been away from Him long enough. I'm very serious about this. You know that everything

I have ever prophesied to you has always come to pass. I plead with you to listen to me."

I was praying on the other end of the phone that my sentiments would somehow lead him to have a change of heart. My prayers took me back to the days when he used to go up to random strangers to talk about God. I longed for him to remember that power. I wanted that chipper boy back more than anyone else did.

Kevin's addiction to heroin was the hindrance that kept my hopes from becoming a reality. The drug problem was also the glare that blinded him to God's understanding. He knew I was telling the truth, but he allowed his desire to be rebelliously independent to block out the sincerity of my words.

"I believe you, Dad, but I'm sorry. I'm just not ready to change. I don't know why. I don't even understand my own actions. Pray for me." I could tell he was beginning to sob, but before I could react and show him my care, he hung up the phone.

The next day I got a call from his aunt informing me that my worst fear had come true. As Kevin was riding his bicycle to get his next fix, he was hit by a drunk driver in a SUV who ran a stop sign. Medical personnel reported that he landed so hard after flying off his bike that parts of his scalp had meshed into the road.

Kevin has yet to receive the blessing of God's calling in his life, simply because he rejected the Lord's understanding. He allowed his parents' lack of concern to be influential in developing his state of rebellion. He neglected the notion that God loves us with a passionate and eternal love that no parent on earth could ever have for us. Kevin didn't have God's understanding and thereby didn't know who he was as God's child. I don't know where he is now, but I pray he has found his way back to the Lord.

What we do defines who we are, and who we are can determine what we'll receive in life. Most people spend their lives wondering why they've had to struggle so much. In some cases, they refuse to come to grips with the fact that who they are is what has hindered them from receiving understanding and the rewards it brings.

Who are you? If you're not an individual focusing on the will of the Lord, parts of your life will confuse you. The key to eradicating this confusion is to seek God and become His servant. Afterward, you must stay on the path He has designed for you, to avoid any uncertainty about whether the will of God is ideal for your life.

For Kevin, heroin was a barrier to him in grabbing onto God's understanding. For you, it may be a marriage, job, or another relationship that isn't of the Lord. When we don't get understanding from God, we must rid ourselves of the obstructions that prevent us from viewing our lives from God's perspective.

As we see with Kevin, becoming the Lord's servant enabled him to receive the knowledge necessary to understand his life. However, his choice to pursue worldly desires made him lose that understanding. Kevin's story is truly disheartening. It shows that we must avoid dismissing God's ways at all costs. The key to maintaining a healthy relationship with God is found in the following promise that God gives to those who obtain understanding:

> *Happy (blessed, fortunate, enviable) is the man who finds skillful and godly Wisdom, and the man who gets understanding [drawing it forth from God's Word and life's*

*experiences], For the gaining of it is better
than the gaining of silver, and the profit of it
better than fine gold.*

Proverbs 3:13-14

When we receive understanding from God, He promises that our lives will be tremendously blessed. But to continue receiving God's insight, we must be obedient to all of His instructions.

If we want to understand, we must faithfully do the will of the Lord. If we say, "I understand," but we're not obedient to what God commands us to do, the perspective we support is our own, not His. We're fooled into acting according to what we think, resulting in a failure to reap the rewards of obtaining God's understanding.

Kevin was burdened, troubled, and in despair because he stopped doing God's will and rejected Godly understanding. According to Psalm 111:10, when we do His will, we understand, and our praise of Him will endure forever. As a result, we won't just praise God out of sacrifice. The peace and satisfaction we'll receive from Him will give birth to a resounding praise from within our hearts. Psalm 119 gives us a key to attaining God's understanding:

*I am Your servant; give me understanding
(discernment and comprehension), that I
may know (discern and be familiar with the
character of) Your testimonies.*

Psalm 119:125

A focus of what I teach as pastor is how to pray to God and how to hear from Him through His Holy Spirit. It is more important to hear God's testimonies, or thoughts concerning a circumstance, than to offer prayers to Him that are filled with fear and doubt. As we allow God's Word to enter our hearts and lives, we will experience His insightful understanding. Once we have *His* Word, we simply need to obey His voice in order to gain the victory.

Most of us want God to do all the work, so we pray, asking Him to fulfill our own heart's desires. Instead, let's gather from the melodic prayer in the above Psalm to realize that we can gain wisdom through prayer regarding how to get God's attention.

Notice the psalmist didn't simply ask God, "Father what are Your testimonies or thoughts about my situation?" Instead, he specifically asked the Lord for the ability to easily understand and discern His perspective. We should pray as the psalmist did. By doing so, we will obtain access to what God really wants us to know about our lives.

> *The entrance and unfolding of Your words*
> *give light; their unfolding gives understanding*
> *(discernment and comprehension) to the*
> *simple.*
>
> Psalm 119:130

We can hear divinely inspired words through many avenues, such as listening to our parents and pastors or by reading the Bible. We are the gatekeepers of our own hearts, allowing or refusing the entrance of God's Word. While the Holy Bible brings about a positive change in the lives of many, others are not affected by God's Word. Either consequence can be the result of the heart's response to what is presented.

As the Lord commands us, we are expected to act according to the Word He gives us. Self-pity, sulking, or any other self-serving temperament can cause us to block out the light that God's Word radiates. Just as all light exposes what hides in darkness, the light of the Word reveals the contents of the dark places in our lives.

Light is expected to benefit all who are in its presence (Matthew 5:14-16). God's words can only give light if we allow those words inside of us. We are also encouraged to share light with others to give them clarity as well. When we allow the Word of God to enter and become part of us, we are enlightened with the understanding we need for our lives.

For example, if the doctor announces that an individual's cancer is now in remission, the entrance of the doctor's words would give light to those who are concerned. The Word of God Almighty can certainly bring more peace than the assurance of a physician. Therefore, trusting God's Word is more important than relying on earthly knowledge.

Jesus even described God's Word as being a seed, needing to *enter* into the ground before becoming productive. He said when the Word is planted in fertile soil, a good measure of fruit is the result. Therefore, those of us who will train our ears to listen and prepare our hearts to receive the Holy Word as seed are also those who will be engulfed by an abundance of God's understanding.

As the following scripture provides, we are influenced by His personality traits that annihilate evil, thereby becoming less like ourselves and more like God Almighty:

> *Let not mercy and kindness [shutting out all*
> *hatred and selfishness] and truth [shutting*

out all deliberate hypocrisy or falsehood]
forsake you; bind them about your neck,
write them upon the tablet of your heart.
So shall you find favor, good understanding,
and high esteem in the sight [or judgment] of
God and man.

Proverbs 3:3-4

As we live in the Lord, mercy, kindness, and truth become our divine qualities. While truth prevents deliberate hypocrisy or falsehood from forming in our hearts, mercy and kindness prevent all hatred and selfishness from becoming a part of our personalities. These attributes reflecting our Creator should be very much an ingredient in our lives.

Once we discipline ourselves to live in the Lord, a character pleasing to God will develop in us, and understanding will grant us a blessed lifestyle of greater ease and sheer enjoyment. Show me someone who's not prosperous and I'll show you someone who doesn't understand. Show me someone whose life has been destroyed through his own disobedience, and I'll show you someone who didn't allow God's Word to enter his life to give light.

My son, if you will receive my words and
treasure up my commandments within you,
Making your ear attentive to skillful and
godly Wisdom and inclining and directing
your heart and mind to understanding
[applying all your powers to the quest for it]

Proverbs 2:1-2

Skillful and Godly wisdom create an entirely new civilization with beneficial laws for us to live by. In some cultures, the benefit is freedom of speech. In other societies, people are given the right to bear arms. As we position our hearts to be receptive of God's understanding, an advantage included in God's way of life is full access to whatever is in His mind regarding our lives.

> *Yes, if you cry out for insight and raise your voice for understanding, If you seek [Wisdom] as for silver and search for skillful and godly Wisdom as for hidden treasures, Then you will understand the reverent and worshipful fear of the Lord and find the knowledge of [our omniscient] God.*
>
> Proverbs 2:3-5

The term *omniscient* in this scripture means that God knows everything. Getting understanding and wisdom lets us find the knowledge God has concerning our lives.

God wants to show how possible the impossible is through His children. Are you someone God can depend on as willing to understand? God wants to change our lives for the better when we consistently seek Him, aiming to accomplish His original intent for our lives. Be one who's submissive to God, yielding and willing to understand the Lord's ways, so you can understand His intended purpose for you to fulfill.

CHAPTER 9
COMMANDING UNDERSTANDING

I had just sat down in my favorite reclining chair with my milk and cookies in front of me, ready to watch cartoons after school. I heard my dad's voice booming from the kitchen.

"Shane, this trash needs to be taken out now."

"Okay, I'll get it," I yelled back to him as I turned once again to my cartoons.

I'll get to it later, I decided.

After all, this was the season premiere of *Batman*, my very favorite after-school show. I finished my cookies and milk and laid on my stomach on the couch.

I heard it before I felt it. First came a whoosh sound like that of a tree limb flying in the air, and I immediately felt the sting across my butt as I flinched. I coiled and turned over. Then I looked up at my father and jerked away from the small tree limb that had just broken across my buttocks.

"I said take out the trash now!" my father yelled, eyeballing me while I scrambled into the kitchen to gather the trash.

I'd forgotten, or rather ignored the fact that a short while before this incident, my father had commanded me to understand his house rules for after school. He told my little sister and me that we weren't free to watch television or enjoy any other activity of leisure until our assigned chores had been completed.

When an authority figure we must submit to commands us to understand, evidently we have the capacity to obey. Even Jesus commanded a group of people to understand what He was teaching. If they didn't have the ability to understand, Jesus would never have commanded it.

> *And He called the people to [Him] again and*
> *said to them, Listen to Me, all of you, and*
> *understand [what I say].*
>
> Mark 7:14

Even as adults, we need to be reminded to understand what's being told to us, because it's easy to become distracted. Many of us do act childishly, only wanting to do what we want to do, when we want to do it, disregarding how others may be affected by our actions. Sometimes we need to be made aware of the commands that we have been given. These commands must be applied to our lives in order for us to build Godly characteristics.

> *My son, forget not my law or teaching, but*
> *let your heart keep my commandments.*
>
> Proverbs 3:1

In chapter three of Proverbs, a father encourages his son to listen intently to all of the lessons he gives. He commands his son to open his heart to understanding, so that his heart may be positioned to hold on to Godly instructions. The next verse in the chapter tells us why.

For length of days and years of a life [worth living] and tranquility [inward and outward and continuing through old age till death], these shall they add to you.

Proverbs 3:2

The father knew what was best for his son. He wanted his son to take heed of his words, because being guided by those words, the father had learned how to live a long and peaceable life. He wanted his son's days and years to be filled with the benefits of understanding that his own life's experience had obtained.

Solomon, the writer of the Proverbs, makes another plea to his son.

My son, keep my words; lay up within you my commandments [for use when needed] and treasure them. Keep my commandments and live, and keep my law and teaching as the apple (the pupil) of your eye. Bind them on your fingers; write them on the tablet of your heart.

Proverbs 7:1-3

In the scripture above, the father is telling his son to keep his commandments and his law as the focus of his life. If children don't make God's understanding a focal point of their lives, it is our responsibility to correct them. When we intentionally or negligently don't share Godly insight with our youth, we place them in jeopardy of following the wrong track.

Whatever constructive criticism we give, most importantly it must be directed by the Holy Spirit and done out of love. My father knew that if he didn't scold me for being disobedient, I'd repeat that selfish act even into my adulthood. I understood that my father wanted me to take out the trash, but I ignored him. In turn, my father had to command me to understand, just as the Bible references how children should be raised.

> *Train up a child in the way he should go: and*
> *when he is old, he will not depart from it.*
> Proverbs 22:6, KJV

When we don't point our children in a Godly direction, we put them at risk of making stupid, worldly decisions. Children must know Who God is in order to know who they are. If we don't teach kids who they are in God, then we leave their quest for identity in the hands of the world. Giving our kids the finest clothes and education isn't enough. Without God as a true point of reference, any upbringing will be in vain.

With respect to the adults who didn't receive Godly teachings when they were children, God looks to us as Christians to guide them in a loving manner. Yet, as much as we may try to lead others in the right direction, it remains that person's responsibility to do his part in obedience. Commanding understanding can only have successful results if the listening party is willing to receive.

I can remember one period of time when my lack of listening led me to no longer want to live. When I was a teenager, I made awful decisions and I felt as if that season of my life would never end. I cried. I prayed, and then I cried some more. I hated hurting God by my crazy, worldly actions. But as much as God and my parents tried to get me to understand that my ways were only hurting myself, I refused to walk in a different direction.

I got to the point where I asked God one night to kill me in my sleep because I didn't feel worthy of my life. When I awoke the next morning, I was disappointed that God hadn't granted my request. The Holy Spirit later told me that God wasn't going to let me off that easy, and that I had work to do for Him.

My teenage years felt like a rat race, with me constantly scurrying after the next worldly desire that everyone else was chasing after. Each race left me in more trouble, yearning to commit my life to God's way. But through those mistakes, I learned the value of trusting God's correction over my own. As much as we may want to use our own understanding to guide our lives, adhering to the guidance of God's commands is the only way we will find true peace in this world.

While many of us may choose to address trouble with our own quick methods of amendment, such haste is usually only motivated by fear or worry. Instead of giving in to the discouraging thoughts that tell us that being patient with the Lord is a pointless feat, we must avoid the desire to act in a hurry. Waiting on the Lord is always worth it.

Waiting and doing nothing seems like the lazy way out, but Who we are waiting on makes a huge difference. When we cease to be busybodies, trying to solve our own problems by scrambling to do this and that, and place total confidence in God as our solution, our understanding of Him gives us rest. We must take command in every situation by understanding our God and His laws.

This discipline of depending only on God's understanding is not an automatic response of human nature. We must consciously restrict ourselves from being involved in the part of our affairs that God has already ordained as His responsibility. Often, what we perceive as a negative circumstance is what God perceives as an opportunity. God creates miracles out of everyday situations, but a miracle can't take place unless we first stand aside. Trust the Lord even with those occurrences you think you can deal with yourself. He can and will handle any state of affairs better than you can, but you have to be willing to allow Him to do the work. God wants the glory! He wants the world to see how great and powerful He is (so others will know to come to Him, too). Let Him demonstrate His glory in your life.

If we try to control our life situations without the Lord's involvement, we won't develop faith or confidence in Him. If we don't trust God, we will yield to the temptation of using our own understanding.

The power of the cross, the same power displayed when Jesus died out of love for His Father and this world, is in you. Use that power to its maximum potential. Through that power, God saves souls and adjusts people's lives every day. How much more can you use that same power to command discouragement, doubt or any other worldly feelings to be still so you may wait upon the Lord to answer completely and respond to what you need?! Command temptation to understand Who your Lord is. Command those around you to understand the same.

When I finally decided that my teenage years would no longer be about disobeying the Lord, I didn't need a great deal of time to learn that I was going to have to do my part. I had to command my life—take charge of my own self—to understand that God, not my flesh, was going to be my Ruler. I had to wise up. I had already admitted that I was dumb, but I got smart by repenting. I asked God, and He gave me His understanding.

Whoever is simple (easily led astray and wavering), let him turn in here! As for him

who lacks understanding, [God's] Wisdom
says to him, Come, eat of my bread and drink
of the [spiritual] wine which I have mixed.

Proverbs 9:4-5

I arrived at a moment when I decided to simply do what I knew was right. This is when I learned to just be honest with myself. I rededicated my life to God in my bedroom and wrote a song about my ordeal.

Some of the lyrics go: "I'm sorry. Please forgive me, Lord. I've known better, and I should be much further up the road. That's why I say, not in this place again will You find me." I had to command an understanding of my own self by saying, "I will not negate my dedication to God. I can't let this ever happen again."

Consider and understand, you stupid ones
among the people! And you [self-confident]
fools, when will you become wise?

Psalm 94:8

Since that time of my rededication, I have been more focused on what matters the most to me now: serving God faithfully in every area of my life. I can't say that I don't have challenges, but I can say that I have grown stronger than those challenges. I've learned how to command my circumstances in order to adhere to God's Word. Wisdom and understanding from God gives us strength beyond that which any of our adversaries can muster or display.

Quite often we'll need to end the associations that are the greatest distractions to our God-centered attention and our overall wellbeing.

Leave off, simple ones [forsake the foolish and simpleminded] and live! And walk in the way of insight and understanding.

Proverbs 9:6

If we're open, desiring God to speak to us directly or through others, when He commands us to live a life of understanding His will and His will only, we'll find ourselves developing a more and more personal and intimate relationship with Him. As a result of our humility before God's will, the worldly desires and fears in our lives will dwindle to nonexistence.

No matter what commands God gives to us, the orders we've received from Him should be carried out with an attitude of full obedience, because of the genuine love we have for God. He loves us, and we know His love is perfect. His love never fails to show us how much He cares for our lives. We can truly rest assured that God doesn't want us to fail. He will not only adorn our lives with the power of understanding, He will also teach us how to use the understanding we've received from Him.

CHAPTER 10
WHAT TO DO WITH UNDERSTANDING

In middle school I didn't have a lot of friends. My social life consisted of church, home, school and more church. One of my classmates, Peter, was the complete opposite. The class broke into applause every time he walked into a room. He had all the coolest clothes and the most friends. And he always had a smile on his face. At least, it seemed that way to those around him. But when he thought no one was looking, I would often see his face turn sad and his eyes solemn. One day, I walked up to him and asked him if he was okay.

"You seem sad all the time," I told him. He looked back at me, his eyes filling with tears. Clearing his throat, he confided in me that his parents were getting a divorce, though it wasn't a big deal. But the expression on his face said that he was devastated.

"You're the only one who noticed," he said, suddenly taking an interest in his shoes.

With understanding, we don't only see what everyone else is looking at, we use understanding to look beyond what's put in front of us and to find out what's really going on behind the veil. Peter was shocked that someone actually cared. He thought that friends were only people who made him feel special or said nice things about him.

> *The rich man is wise in his own eyes*
> *and conceit, but the poor man who has*
> *understanding will find him out.*
>
> Proverbs 28:11

When you have understanding, you'll look past what everyone else sees and discern what is real behind the facade. We need God's understanding, but we also need to learn what to do with it. Having understanding isn't a pass to bring judgment on others. Understanding adjusts the lens on your eyes so that you can see what was previously hidden.

Although we should immediately acknowledge the gift of God's understanding, our pride often leads us to do otherwise. Thus, because of our disobedience, many of us aren't as far along in God's plan as we should be. Let's look then at some practical ways that the Bible shows us regarding what to do with the understanding we get. After obediently applying these lessons to our lives, we are certain to attain success and receive positive results.

Once we're graced with a favorable outcome, it's only natural to give God the genuine praise that's due to Him.

> *For God is the King of all the earth;*
> *sing praises in a skillful psalm and with*
> *understanding.*
>
> Psalm 47:7

How often do we stand in a church service singing to God, but we're only reciting the lyrics from our mouths, not singing from our hearts? We're praising out of memory, or singing what we rehearsed at worship practice a few days before. When you sing and praise God with understanding, however, your mind is in complete alignment with the Lord's perfect will for your life. You ignore thoughts that lead you to mentally wander down a path other than the Lord's. You humbly submit to God's will, knowing that He will take care of you in a loving manner, no matter what. All of you is given to God through your praises. You aren't pondering about the traffic on the way to church, your job assignments from that week or the social event you went to the night before. Your mind is completely and utterly focused on the Lord, as you engulf yourself in His peaceful presence. Be true in your praises to the Lord. Give Him all you have through praise, not just on Sunday morning, but during the entire week.

As we begin to give the Lord praise and glory, He will begin to build, repair and establish His perfect will in many areas of our lives.

> *The Lord by skillful and godly Wisdom has founded the earth; by understanding He has established the heavens.*
>
> Proverbs 3:19

This scripture tells us that understanding establishes. When you have established desires from God's perspective, they are solidified. No one then, except you, yourself, can hold you back from achieving your aims because they are made concrete by being aligned with God's will.

We've all had dreams, whether they're of owning a small business, having a lucrative job or starting a non-profit. Think of what happens when you attach understanding to those dreams. As understanding establishes, it gives you the assurance that you can stake your dreams on God's insight. God Himself used understanding to establish the very heavens. How much more then can we use understanding to establish what God has spoken into our lives?

When understanding is used to establish, we must then continue to seek out and receive understanding so that we can always be led on the right path.

> *The wise also will hear and increase in learning, and the person of understanding will acquire skill and attain to sound counsel [so that he may be able to steer his course rightly].*
>
> Proverbs 1:5

When we obtain understanding in all that we do, we have the ability to make clear decisions about our lives. Whether we're faced with uncertainty or opportunity, understanding helps us make choices that are pleasing to God. By satisfying God's desires, we are able to travel down the road of peace and security that comes with the presence of the Holy Spirit.

The key to traveling along the proper path is through obedience to God. Though some people may want to be pitied when they receive instruction that they don't like, or that is different from their own thoughts, obtaining the counsel available by way of understanding requires accepting insight with no reservations or restrictions. A person who takes in understanding with appreciation will be able to steer his course rightly.

> *[Discretion shall watch over you, understanding shall keep you] to deliver you from the alien woman, from the outsider with her flattering words,*
>
> *Who forsakes the husband and guide of her youth and forgets the covenant of her God.*
>
> *For her house sinks down to death and her paths to the spirits [of the dead].*
>
> Proverbs 2:16-18

The passage above is a warning of what can happen when we don't use understanding. In this example, God's understanding can keep us away from people who would seduce us into doing wrong with flattering words while getting us to disregard the promises that God has made to us in exchange for our lives. Understanding can keep those people at bay.

In addition to distancing sins away from our lives, we can use understanding to live a life of victory. The following scripture highlights that achievement comes to those who don't abandon the understanding they've been given.

> *He who gains Wisdom loves his own life; he who keeps understanding shall prosper and find good.*
>
> Proverbs 19:8

We can easily relish the wisdom we receive from a newfound revelation, but how often do we go on to practice the life-changing truths that we receive? The Word of God is the understanding to be planted in our hearts. If the understanding isn't rooted deep inside of us, it'll be swept away in the rain of a stormy situation. Understanding must remain at the forefront of our minds so that it can be applied immediately when situations emerge.

With God's understanding fixed in our hearts, we can have massive successes in our lives. If success wanes, it's not because God has lead us astray, it's because we have strayed away from His understanding. If we have temporary understanding, we'll have temporary success.

Many benefits accrue to getting and using understanding. The resulting prosperity can potentially mount to a point where others are jealous of our ability to make prudent choices. We may even find ourselves envied by not only those in less fortunate positions but by the billionaire business owner.

While money can bring us temporary satisfaction, being financially wealthy doesn't always mean that we have the wisdom to use those assets correctly.

> *Happy (blessed, fortunate, enviable) is the man who finds skillful and godly Wisdom, and the man who gets understanding [drawing it forth from God's Word and life's experiences],*
>
> *For the gaining of it is better than the gaining of silver, and the profit of it better than fine gold.*
>
> Proverbs 3:13-14

One of the vital steps you should take when you get understanding is to explain it to those who don't have it yet. If you have what it takes to stand out in the workplace, you can explain to someone else how to achieve that status because you have the insight to do so. When you see someone slacking off in school, help him to understand the consequences of his poor performance. If you perceive that this individual doesn't comprehend your explanation, go into further detail. Explanation is the impartation of understanding.

God doesn't want to give us His understanding just so we can have the knowledge in our possession. He wants us to pray for others who also need His understanding. It's God's good pleasure to give us what we require to minister to the needs of His people. Instead of praying for astonishing biblical revelation, pray that God will speak to His people in the best possible way, telling them exactly what they need to know. Praying for others allows God to tell us what to reveal to those we pray for, so that they might have understanding as well. When we pray to find out God's instruction for every situation and intercede according to His Word, we become well prepared to share God's understanding in a spiritual form.

When we possess understanding, we have the abilities to discern what is true, protect what is precious, guide what is lost and minister to those who are helpless. Using understanding in our everyday lives is indeed enjoyable, and we should seek God to gain even more. What will we do with the understanding God gives us? Let's make a conscious effort to learn how to respond instinctively, with understanding being the answer to each of life's questions.

CHAPTER 11
THE HABIT OF UNDERSTANDING

I don't remember the last time I received a ticket for driving over the speed limit. Sadly, though, I wasn't always such a law-abiding citizen. I used to look over my shoulder every minute, hoping a highway patrol officer wouldn't track me. If I saw a police car while I was speeding, I would slam on my brakes.

With my speedometer steadily climbing, the Holy Spirit asked me if I would go to Heaven if Jesus came back that very second. I was speeding, breaking the law, and I knew it. Looking at the cars in the lanes around me, I thought, *everybody else is speeding. Of course I'd go to Heaven.*

The Holy Spirit responded, "You're doing wrong, you know you're doing wrong and you're intentionally doing wrong. Would you go to Heaven if Jesus came back right now?"

His words stung to the core of my soul. Convicted by the Holy Spirit, I committed myself to make following the speed limit a habit. I understood that even the smallest of intentional wrongs could land me in Hell, and I wasn't prepared to spend an eternity away from Christ for a few fleeting moments on the highway.

In order to live for God, you must create certain habits in your life. You must make it a habit to read His Word, to pray and to obey Him daily, even in the smallest of areas.

The very concept of "habit," of course, the word, has earned a bad reputation. This misrepresentation causes people to avoid creating habits in their lives that would be valuable. Unfortunately, people equate the idea of habits with a negative part of their lifestyles, when, in all actuality, a habit can also be quite positive. Habits can become an integral part of our personality and overall identity.

One of the most beneficial habits we can commit to is to make a practice of asking God for His understanding. It's imperative that we adopt a habit of getting understanding from God concerning every aspect of our lives, so that we can carry out His will and be of assistance to others.

In order to maintain understanding as a habit, we have to surround ourselves with people who have the same intention. God spoke this to me: "Time brings influence. Influence gives birth to decisions. Decisions father every action, and every action has a result." After some time, each of our friends has the ability to affect our actions through the influence we have allowed them over us. If we make a habit of surrounding ourselves with foolish people, we ourselves will soon become equally foolish. If we constantly surround ourselves with those who seek God's insight, we will become wise.

> *Say to skillful and godly Wisdom, You are my sister, and regard understanding or insight as your intimate friend— that they may keep you from the loose woman, from*

the adventuress who flatters with and makes
smooth her words.

Proverbs 7:4-5

We form habits when we engage in close relationships with others. A boyfriend and girlfriend may make a habit of spending time together after school, learning more about each other and drawing nearer. A married couple will be in constant communication, updating each other on the progress of their day and leaning on each other for encouragement. Similarly, we need to have a close relationship with wisdom and understanding, habitually gleaning insight and knowledge that will help us to succeed.

My mouth shall speak wisdom; and
the meditation of my heart shall be
understanding.

Psalm 49:3

How long is the meditation of one's heart? It's consistent—habitual. Like the meditation of our hearts, the Word should be a part of our daily walk with God. The Bible is essential to making God's understanding habitual because in it lies the central structure for our lives. If your habits are only built on a worldly foundation, then they lack a constructive support system. Use scriptures daily, throughout your everyday problems. When trouble arises, speak life into your situation, not anger.

He who is slow to anger has great understanding, but he who is hasty of spirit exposes and exalts his folly.

Proverbs 14:29

A person who has a great understanding of God's insight will always be slow to anger. Conversely, a person who is quick to become irritated or ill-tempered is only promoting his own recklessness. People like this would rather go by emotions than by prayer. The Bible says that in *all* of our ways, we should acknowledge God and He will direct our paths (Proverbs 3:6).

If we are slow to anger, it's because we have learned to be quick to understand. Make it a habit to seek God for His understanding no matter what the problem, situation or circumstance is. Why become angry if someone is making absurd comments about you? Simply understand that fools say foolish things. They're supposed to, just like dogs are supposed to bark.

The closer you are to understanding, the more you can focus on God and not the frustration of the situation. No matter what arises, you will be well prepared to not let emotions get the best of your mentality. You will easily remember that no circumstance is worth your peace. Having focus like this will prepare you for any season of your life.

And of Issachar, men who had understanding of the times to know what Israel ought to do, 200 chiefs; and all their kinsmen were under their command

1 Chronicles 12:32

When we make understanding a habit, we can know what to do at any given point in time. The men in the scripture above had an understanding of the times and they knew exactly what to do during that season. God has this world in a flow of seasons, all of them moving and stopping at specific intervals. Think about the flow of traffic, which consists of travel, pauses and fast and slow traveling zones. When our season presents us with a red traffic light, we have no reason to become discouraged. Don't be jealous of the opposing traffic moving right along. Realize that your time is coming, your season, too, is just ahead.

How do we know what to do in a particular season? We must have an understanding that we have to habitually hear God. The Bible says that God gives knowledge to the ones who have understanding (Daniel 2:21).

How do I personally know what to do in a situation? I've gained the understanding that I must hear God concerning *every* circumstance. Listening for God's guidance has become a habit of mine. I became frustrated with my failing ways, so I had to discipline myself to seek out and wait on God's Word. That way, I could apply God's insight to the situation before it had an opportunity to become an ordeal. Sitting patiently may seem to be in vain, but waiting on the Lord is always better than rushing out to do your own will, only to find you've really messed up.

Make a habit of understanding that God controls the flow of traffic in our lives. God isn't going to jump off His throne to orchestrate our lives, however. He relies on our obedience. God is the One Who commands, and we obey on all levels of understanding.

CHAPTER 12
FIVE LEVELS OF UNDERSTANDING

Many people have no or little understanding of their lives, despite naively thinking they know more than they actually do. Others in this world may have perfect understanding, but lack the wisdom to properly apply that understanding to their lives. As the Holy Spirit Himself has showed me in the Word, exactly five different levels of understanding will help followers of Christ to accurately identify where their relationship stands with God.

We can't better our lives until we understand what our problems are. Once we obtain understanding, we'll know how to specifically pray about which personality traits need the most improvement.

Are you one who encourages *others* in faith, but you have difficulties allowing the Lord to build *you* when times become frustrating? Do you read and believe the Word of the Lord, but forget to apply the scriptures to your life when troubles arise? Do you find yourself to be slow to anger in public, but become easily infuriated with those close to you? Perhaps the solution is to obtain the understanding needed.

God doesn't want us to only have peace with others, He wants us to love ourselves. However, to love ourselves, we must first know ourselves.

At one point in time, I didn't know how quickly my anger could escalate. But I was sitting in class one day when I was in the eighth grade, and for some reason I felt frustrated. I don't even remember why, but I felt disrespected by my teacher, and I responded with pure outrage. My teacher called my father that evening, and let's just say that after he disciplined me, I created no further interruptions for her. I needed to increase my relationship with understanding because I often found myself easily angered by those around me. Through God's grace, I learned how to obtain *perfect understanding* to keep me from making the same foolish mistakes over again.

Knowing what level of understanding we have from God's perspective will allow us to pray according to the areas of our lives that need attention, thereby becoming better Christians and advancing the love we have for ourselves. The following are the five levels of understanding: *no understanding, your own understanding, good understanding, great understanding,* and *perfect understanding.* As we examine each level, we will learn the necessary components involved in becoming well acquainted with the highest level of understanding, *perfect understanding.*

Level 1: No Understanding

Those who don't follow God's Law are separated from Him and have no understanding. Where there is *no understanding,* sin abounds. Level one is a dangerous place to be because God will continue to correct us until we climb to the next level of understanding. Those who have no understanding are very wise in how to do what's wrong. For such people, sinning comes easy, and doing what's right seems hard.

> *Then I said, Surely these are only the poor; they are [sinfully] foolish and have no understanding, for they know not the way of the Lord, the judgment (the just and righteous law) of their God.*
>
> Jeremiah 5:4

God's law is His way of conducting life on Earth. Those who are sinfully foolish and don't know the way of the Lord have no understanding. God is a loving Father Who longs to be closer to us all, but sin separates God from mankind. When we are distant from God, we are void of understanding and unable to experience the love, joy and freedom that come from having fellowship with Him. We need to look at God as Someone with a personality, Who treats us not as Creator to creature, but as Father to child.

When it comes to God, it's all about relationship. All He wants is fellowship with His children. The only way to get to God is through Jesus, not through any rituals or routines. Following God's law keeps us in great relationship with our Father.

Level 2: Your Own Understanding

Emotions have a tendency to drive us to act contrary to God's will for us. Responding to life according to how we feel is so much easier than taking the approach God declares. The only way we should act, however, is in the manner God wants, and that takes self-discipline.

*Lean on, trust in, and be confident in the
Lord with all your heart and mind and do not
rely on your own insight or understanding.*

Proverbs 3:5

Any understanding that God hasn't given us that we claim ownership of is our own understanding. We have to trust in and rely on God with all of our hearts. Trusting God with ninety percent of our hearts isn't sufficient. God isn't a prostitute, that we should use Him to feel better about a circumstance and then let Him go. We have to dedicate 100 percent of our lives to the Lord. People treat God like a prostitute because they don't want to make a commitment to Him. Instead, they want the instant pleasures of worldly desires.

Level 3: Good Understanding

Good understanding is of a man's intellectual nature. Those who possess good understanding greatly honor and respect the Lord in their worship. They know the Word of God, and they have received a form of understanding, but only on a cognitive level.

*Let not mercy and kindness [shutting out all
hatred and selfishness] and truth [shutting
out all deliberate hypocrisy or falsehood]
forsake you; bind them about your neck,
write them upon the tablet of your heart.
So shall you find favor, good understanding,
and high esteem in the sight [or judgment] of
God and man.*

Proverbs 3:3-4

Having mercy and being kind toward others from the heart, with boldness in proclaiming the truth despite the circumstances, is demonstrated by a person with good understanding. These qualities are not only beneficial to those we treat decently in this way, but they also provide assistance to us during life's stressful moments.

One of those stressful moments for me occurred when I opened a foreclosure notice for my house that had come in the mail. Hands shaking, I told God that I believed in His ability to provide the means to be able to pay the mortgage. "I don't want the blessing one second before You want to give it to me," I said. I truly wanted for my will to be aligned with His.

In church the next day, I told my congregation about my trust in God to meet my financial obligation, using it as an example of how their faith should be. I felt very comfortable in telling them because it would help strengthen the congregants' faith in God. Everyone seemed inspired by my openness and boldness of conviction.

About a week later, one of the church's frequent visitors scheduled a meeting with me. I had no clue what he wanted to meet about, but my thoughts were leaning toward the fact that he now wanted to join the church instead of being a faithful visitor. After some small talk, however, he got right to the point of his visit. He told me that he'd been praying for me when he heard me tell the story about my mortgage.

He asked if I would be willing to share how far behind I was in my mortgage payments and the amount of money that I needed. I told him that I appreciated his concern but the amount was exorbitant. I hesitantly told him that the amount due was close to $5,000.

"Whoa!" he exclaimed.

I chuckled, thanking him for his consideration.

"But, Pastor, that's the exact amount God told me to give you."

I blinked. Many thoughts raced through my head, but the thought that was clear was my utter astonishment at God's great love and power.

"When I prayed and asked God to bless you to pay your mortgage, He said to me, 'Why are you asking Me to bless him when you have the money to give him? Give him $5,000." I'm shocked that I heard from God exactly what you needed. God has never used me like that before."

Instead of being stressed or upset, I held on to God's understanding concerning the mortgage, proclaiming to my congregation His promise to take care of me. The love that God showed me because I received His understanding was astounding.

Continuing on the path to the highest level of understanding, we can observe those who have great understanding by their attitudes.

Level 4: Great Understanding

A good temperament transfers us from good understanding to great understanding.

> *He who is slow to anger has great understanding, but he who is hasty of spirit exposes and exalts his folly.*
>
> Proverbs 14:29

The person with great understanding has insight that subdues anger. To climb to a level of great understanding, we can't be quick to respond with hostility. Have you ever gotten angry about a situation before getting the understanding? I remember growing up and hearing random outbursts that could have been avoided, had the understanding been received.

One day, I heard my father's voice booming throughout the house.

"Who left the light on in the kitchen?" he yelled.

Everyone froze. We all knew that the next person to leave the lights on in the house would be dealt with.

"Who was it?" he thundered.

My voice trembled.

"Um, Dad, you just came from the kitchen two minutes ago. That was you."

Dad turned around and turned back with an incredulous look on his face.

"Uh-oh. I sure did leave that light on." He picked up his cereal bowl and sat on the couch. "Oh, sorry about that," he said.

Imagine the friction that could be avoided if we were slow to anger while getting understanding in lieu of flying into a state of rage. Before jumping to conclusions, we can avoid being unnecessarily angry about a potentially upsetting situation. Always get the understanding first.

Level 5: Perfect Understanding

Perfect understanding shows up when we have our ears attentive to the words proceeding from God's mouth, to the point where nothing in the world is disturbing or distracting us. We're so attracted to what God is saying that we don't care what's happening around us. Understanding *perfectly* is the key to truly knowing and recognizing God's divine plan for our lives.

I had to have perfect understanding when my dad was given some distressing news at the hospital. According to the scans, he would need to have quadruple bypass surgery because four of his arteries were almost completely blocked. My dad stared blankly at the doctor's desk, and my older sister rubbed my dad's back for comfort. As we looked at the clock, it seemed as if we were waiting for hours to hear the doctor's conclusion as to the course of treatment we should take. The doctor interrupted the clock's ticking concert with his recommendation that the surgery be performed that very day. My dad was immediately rushed into the operating room.

More ticking. More waiting.

I hurried to my car, turning up my collar against the wind. Countless thoughts raced through my head. What if something happened to my dad on the operating table? What if the surgeon made a mistake?

Tired of all of the speculation, I asked God out loud, facing my biggest fear.

"God, is my father going to die?"

What He said back to me caused me to perfectly understand what was happening.

God said, "I'm not preparing you for death. I'm preparing you for life. This is just another part of life you haven't experienced yet."

I held onto that Word like I'd never held onto anything else before. I hurried back to the hospital, and I repeated to my mother and sisters what God had told me in the car. My family was relieved to finally have peace about their Pop Wall.

Some people lose their focus on what God has spoken. The fault comes when they stop hearing God and start listening to other sources. When we give up on hearing what God wants, we quit altogether. Oftentimes, quitting leads us to decide that our ways are even better than God's. In such instances, God may respond to us in anger.

> *The anger of the Lord shall not turn back until He has executed and accomplished the thoughts and intents of His mind and heart. In the latter days you shall consider and understand it perfectly.*
>
> Jeremiah 23:20

As we see in this instance of the Bible, many times God has become wrathful because His people don't listen. Even though God is slow to anger, He often uses anger as a means to lead His children to repent and fall back into a state of obedience. Therefore, as we read this scripture in the latter days of now, we can have perfect understanding about why God's responses turned into fury. When we don't listen, that same perfect understanding can be applied to our own situations in life.

God is disappointed in the disobedience of a child. When God's children refuse to listen to His plans, He is often angered by our lack of awareness. When we experience the result of God's anger, instead of placing our thoughts on the negative situations that we're facing, we should focus on the fact that He is trying to get our attention. When our minds are in the right place, we can notice that the negative situations have quieted us, brought us back to God, and now He has our attention. In repentance, we go back to obeying the commands that He originally gave us. Perfect understanding sees the entire picture, from the command, to the disobedience, to the consequence.

We *choose* to have perfect understanding by hearing what God says. In perfect understanding, we know that whether God responds to our actions in anger or approval, He's doing so out of love. In perfect understanding, we don't allow thoughts counteractive to the Word of God to penetrate our minds. We are firmly planted in the truth that His love is all we need. We easily dismiss everything else without hesitation. Whatever God says, that's what we understand. We don't think about it, or mull it over: we're focused only on hearing and obeying what God says. We don't have to evaluate or calculate —we simply believe and obey.

We have to stay attentive to what God has said. He already knows what's going on in the present, and He knows the future. He knew about every circumstance that would arise before He said, "Let there be light."

Don't look at where you are right now. Look forward to what God sees in the future, where He's already worked everything out. What have you been involved in where God hasn't come through for you? Doesn't He always take care of you? If you want to increase your satisfaction in life, you have to get an understanding, and most frequently you'll receive understanding during prayer.

CHAPTER 13
PRAYING FOR UNDERSTANDING

*Moreover, as for me, far be it from me that
I should sin against the Lord by ceasing to
pray for you; but I will instruct you in the
good and right way.*

1 Samuel 12:23

It's a sin not to pray. By praying, I don't mean saying your prayers when you get up in the morning. Prayer should be a lifestyle. Our whole life should center on our relationship with God. Whenever a negative situation arises in our lives, our first instinct should be to pray for understanding. We must ask God for His insight about each circumstance we face in order to know how to best handle the problem at hand. While asking God for His input, it's important to also ask Him how to pray for what we are dealing with. Don't just pray what you want. Pray what God wants. That way, the result will always be a "yes" answer.

If you have confusion in your household, don't just pray for it to be removed. Ask God what His understanding of the situation is and *how* He desires you to pray about what your home is going through. In many instances, God Himself may want the confusion to stay, not because He loves confusion, but because He is allowing something greater to arise from it. That something greater could be an incentive for your loved ones to come together in love, pray more or even to bring some dark behaviors into the light.

If you automatically pray for the confusion to be removed simply because you don't understand its purpose, then you run the risk of praying against God's will. This is why you must first pray for the understanding of every circumstance, so that you can view the trouble from God's all-knowing perspective.

The correct understanding always comes from God and His Word. Once we get understanding from the Lord, His promise is that we will benefit from His knowledge in every way He makes available to us. From His insight, we will have a sound judgment of how to manage our problems, and a viewpoint that is directly aligned with His knowledge. To receive such divine discernment, our principal role is to act as fervent, hungry servants of the Kingdom.

> Let my mournful cry and supplication come [near] before You, O Lord; give me understanding (discernment and comprehension) according to Your word [of assurance and promise].
>
> Psalm 119:169

Like the psalmist who penned this verse, we must be so hungry for the knowledge of the Lord to penetrate into our beings that it makes us passionately cry out to Him. We must be desperate for God's understanding and Word for every situation. God will honor this passion because of its sincerity. He may respond by placing us into His loving presence or He may answer our cries by immediately granting us the understanding we are yearning for. If the Lord chooses to allow you to patiently wait for an answer, be grateful and humbly stay still in His peaceful presence. Don't act until you have His understanding.

Many have prayed and asked God for things, and He doesn't give it to them because they don't have the understanding for it. Giving to His children isn't hard for God. After all, everything in the world is His to give. Instead of saying, "I need a car," pray, "Father, give me the understanding for a car." Instead of saying, "I have more bills than I do income," pray, "Father, give me the understanding for these bills." Often, people get cars, jobs and money without God's consent. Because they haven't asked for His understanding, they lack the ability to manage what they have with Godly wisdom. Unfortunately, this leaves them later feeling that that their new car, job or whatever else has provided them with more headaches than benefits.

If you have a bill that you can't afford to pay, receiving the money for its payment will only provide you with temporary relief. On the other hand, understanding how you got yourself into that situation in the first place and being blessed with the wisdom to avoid such a scenario in the future will keep you from making the same mistake again later on. Seek God's understanding, not things.

After receiving an understanding in prayer, know that God's will is greater than your own by believing with genuine faith that the Lord will take care of you. Jesus wants us to have the faith of a little child. We have to become innocent. You can tell kids that the tooth fairy is coming to pick up their tooth, and they will barely sleep because of their anticipation. They really want Santa Claus to eat those cookies that they put out for him on Christmas Eve. Their faith and expectation in what they've been told has no shred of doubt or unbelief. What they hear is what they promptly take in as truth.

Similar to children, we must trust God's Word the instant that He speaks it. He has already promised to take care of you as His child, so all there is left to do is to believe.

We think too much about if God is going to pull through for us instead of trusting Him beyond a doubt. We have to realize that God is giving us the opportunity to come before Him in prayer, and He'll completely satisfy our needs. Some people are in a state of lack because God can't trust them with what He wants to give them. Why would God give someone a thousand dollars if she hasn't proved her ability to properly manage one hundred dollars?

The understanding that we have determines whether God will answer our prayers —or not. I would never give an iPad to a four-month-old to play with. The baby doesn't have the understanding. In the same way, God wouldn't be inclined to give a new car to someone who doesn't know how to drive. That person doesn't understand the rules of the road, putting everyone near the vehicle in danger.

If you look around you and observe what you have, you'll see that your possessions are on the level that you understand. The same can be said for the job you have, the clothes you're wearing and the knowledge in your head. For your protection, God will keep you in the place that is aligned with what you understand. To have more given to you, you must come to the point in your life at which you choose to be desperate for God's understanding. Then, you can be raised to a level where you can be a blessing to His people and to the world. It's God's great pleasure to give us the desires of our hearts. As we get more understanding, God will raise us to higher levels.

After spending time in prayer and desiring God's understanding, we won't be as hungry for material possessions. Earthly goods come as an aftermath of the glorious experience that accompanies spending time with God. When we pray for possessions, our heart is in and for those possessions. Praying for understanding is praying for God's will and knowledge concerning every situation, tugging at the heart of God and leaning on His will and guidance.

In the Bible, Daniel was known as a man who prayed three times a day. He would open his window and cry out to God. Daniel had a special request for God but he didn't get an answer until three weeks later.

> *Then he said to me, Fear not, Daniel, for from the first day that you set your mind and heart to understand and to humble yourself before your God, your words were heard, and I have come as a consequence of [and in response to] your words.*
>
> *But the prince of the kingdom of Persia withstood me for twenty-one days. Then Michael, one of the chief [of the celestial] princes, came to help me, for I remained there with the kings of Persia.*
>
> *Now I have come to make you understand what is to befall your people in the latter days, for the vision is for [many] days yet to come.*
>
> Daniel 10:12-14

After three weeks, an angel told Daniel that because he humbled himself and sought God for understanding, God would finally give Daniel what he had been praying for. Because of his patience, God granted Daniel the understanding of what was going to happen to the people in his kingdom.

Sincere prayers for understanding will always be heard by God. Prayer produces understanding. But God will never conform to our understanding. Move from praying for the desires of your heart to praying for the desires of God's heart. He wants us to completely replace our thoughts with His. What we must pray for is that God will give us His insight, not our own.

When we pray God's desires, we have to immediately have faith that God has already sent an answer. Like Daniel's prayer, an answer may take a while to reach us, but if it's God's will, then it's definitely on the way. Having patience in our prayer lives is a part of submitting to God's purpose for us. With every prayer, we must tell the Lord, "Father, I don't want anything You have to give me one second before You are ready." When we allow our desires to die, we show God that we trust His perfect timing, no matter what our personal plans may be.

Once we have prayed, we don't have to deal with the situation any longer — the situation is being dealt with by God Himself. You've given it to the Father God Almighty. If fear comes, literally *tell* the fear to go see God. If worry comes, literally tell the worry to go see God. Whenever the devil tries to discourage my day, I talk back to him. I say, "Devil, I don't even know why you're bothering me. I don't have my life anymore. Go talk to Jesus!" We must tell the negatives of our lives to go bother the One Who has our lives, Jesus.

Since you have no need to worry if God has your life, you have no need to worry if God has your problems. Your problems are no longer your own, they are the Lord's.

In the Bible, Solomon became king over all of Israel. At the time, Israel had so many people living there that the population couldn't be counted. Solomon recognized that he needed understanding so that he could rule God's people justly and faithfully. So, he asked for God's understanding.

> *Now, O Lord my God, You have made Your servant king instead of David my father, and I am but a lad [in wisdom and experience]; I know not how to go out (begin) or come in (finish).*
>
> *Your servant is in the midst of Your people whom You have chosen, a great people who cannot be counted for multitude.*
>
> *So give Your servant an understanding mind and a hearing heart to judge Your people, that I may discern between good and bad. For who is able to judge and rule this Your great people?*
>
> *It pleased the Lord that Solomon had asked this.*
>
> *God said to him, Because you have asked this and have not asked for long life or for riches, nor for the lives of your enemies, but have asked for yourself understanding to recognize what is just and right,*
>
> *Behold, I have done as you asked. I have given you a wise, discerning mind, so that no*

one before you was your equal, nor shall any
arise after you equal to you.

1 Kings 3:7-12

An impulse to do wrong comes from a lack of understanding. The reason that people sin is because they don't have an understanding about their destructive habits. Without understanding, keeping God's law is difficult. Those who receive understanding from the Lord have a strong-minded desire to continuously do His will. When you haven't heard His heart or His will concerning what He wants you to do, it's easier to fall for the devil's schemes.

Give me understanding, that I may keep
Your law; yes, I will observe it with my whole
heart.

Psalm 119:34

Satan thrives on ignorance and fear. We can destroy Satan's kingdom by using understanding to erase ignorance. When you *understand* God's will for every situation you face, no form of discouragement can knock you down. Having God's direction is the key to defeating the enemy. Understanding becomes most useful when you actually apply the knowledge to your life, allowing it to be a shield against the devil's attacks.

The more you pray for understanding, the more you can begin to see yourself winning every test the enemy tries to throw at you. Watch God follow through with every prayer you ask as you continuously allow yourself to pray for situations according to His perfect design for your life. It's time-out, though, for people standing under their own thoughts and desires. I stand under

God. I stand under His will. I stand under His direction —I understand.

Prayer for Understanding

Our Father, we thank You that you have made Your understanding available for us so that we won't lean to our own understanding. Give us Your understanding for every area of our lives.

We need You because Your direction is the guide we choose for our lives. If we don't receive a Word from You, we will be still until we do. We know how dangerous it is to act according to our own will instead of seeking You for the path we need to take.

Thank You, Father, for always taking perfectly great care of us, even when we aren't as close to You, obeying You, as we should be. We humble ourselves to Your Holy Spirit, so that He can lead, guide and direct our lives as we receive wisdom and understanding from You.

We desire to give You and only You the glory, praise and honor You deserve. In Jesus' name we pray. Amen.

CHAPTER 14
WISDOM AND UNDERSTANDING

Happy (blessed, fortunate, enviable) is the man who finds skillful and godly Wisdom, and the man who gets understanding [drawing it forth from God's Word and life's experiences], For the gaining of it is better than the gaining of silver, and the profit of it better than fine gold.

Proverbs 3:13-14

It was Friday night, December 23, 1983, and I was fifteen years old. This would be the very first time I would preach in a church and to a congregation, a far cry from acting like a preacher when I was a child. My mother was the head of the missionary department in our church, and she'd asked me to preach for a service that the missionaries were hosting. I said I would do it, but I was extremely nervous from the time I was asked onward.

To top it all off, the youth pastor of the church, whom I greatly admired, was the one introducing me. He really boosted me in his introduction with all types of accolades, and the crowd was very excited to hear the message I was about to deliver. As I stepped up to the microphone, the crowd gazing directly at me with smiles, cheering and praising God, I noticed something. Preaching in front of people was so very different than what I had imagined. All the wisdom people declared that I possessed as a would-be preacher wasn't the same as understanding how to deliver what I knew.

I kept my head down, reading my message for almost the entirety of my time behind the podium. I was too nervous to look at the assembly. When I finished, I said, "God bless you." Even though I received lots of hugs and compliments from the congregants after the service, I was not 100 percent pleased with how I ministered.

Had I known then what I know now, I would have spent the same time I used emulating other preachers and applied those moments toward praying for God's insight to direct my career path. Had I done that, I would have had God's understanding of how to deliver my sermon that night. It wasn't enough for me to be wise about what other preachers did when they were ministering, I had to gain the understanding that would cause me to be the minister God had called *me* to be.

We can have wisdom, but not have understanding. Without wisdom, understanding is impossible to attain. God is the only One we should get our wisdom from. Once we ask for wisdom from the Lord, a request for understanding should always follow. Who has given us the wisdom we have? Is it wisdom itself who is the giver? Is truth the one who has given us wisdom?

Proverbs is one of the greatest books of wisdom, filled with profound truths. These fragments of insight are given to us so that we will know Godly wisdom and be able to comprehend what He wants us to understand.

He who gains Wisdom loves his own life; he who keeps understanding shall prosper and find good.

Proverbs 19:8

According to the scripture above, wisdom is what saves our lives from foolishness, keeping us clear of all heinous activities and pitfalls. If we don't study and practice wisdom, we'll be in a place where we aren't receptive to what God offers.

Without the use of understanding, however, wisdom results in no action at all. A scholar could memorize the entire book of Proverbs word for word, but if he doesn't put any of it into action, then his knowledge lacks proper understanding. God's Word is full of wisdom, but can only be of positive use to us if we decide to put it into action as a formal part of our lives. It's not okay to know scriptures by heart but still lash out in anger or act selfishly toward others. A person full of understanding would take all of that knowledge and implement it in his daily life.

What are we doing to ensure that God's wisdom is applied to our lives? God didn't provide the Bible so that it could collect dust. He gave it to us so that His knowledge could be put into proper effect in our lives. If our mouths speak God's wisdom, yet we intentionally sin, we will live guilt-ridden lives of failure, and not of faith. Every word spoken isn't always a result of a heart that's totally committed to living according to God's understanding. Instead, words are oftentimes spoken from self-centered goals and desires that aren't aligned with God's plan for our lives.

> *My mouth shall speak wisdom; and the meditation of my heart shall be understanding.*
>
> Psalm 49:3, KJV

Whenever we don't acquire our words and understanding from God, the source is always something else, whether it be our own thoughts or the enemy's. So many people can talk a good game, but their hearts are far from what is coming out of their mouths. They can speak the church lingo, and they can talk about Jesus, but the concentration of their hearts contrasts with their actions. What then is the understanding that their hearts are meditating on? Their hearts are focused on someone else's understanding, not God's.

Looking at their lives, is that the kind of wisdom you want to have? Speaking from our own minds is dangerous. It's how cliques and cults are formed every day. As people listen to the demonic teachings that are indoctrinated by cult leaders, they believe something that God has no part in. Let your understanding be of God and your wisdom be of Christ Who strengthens you. No other source is necessary.

> *Wisdom is the principal thing; therefore get wisdom: and with all thy getting get understanding.*
>
> Proverbs 4:7, KJV

> *My son, if you will receive my words and treasure up my commandments within you,*
> *Making your ear attentive to skillful and godly Wisdom and inclining and directing*

*your heart and mind to understanding
[applying all your powers to the quest for it];
Yes, if you cry out for insight and raise
your voice for understanding,
If you seek [Wisdom] as for silver and
search for skillful and godly Wisdom as for
hidden treasures,
Then you will understand the reverent
and worshipful fear of the Lord and find the
knowledge of [our omniscient] God.*

Proverbs 2:1-5

*The proverbs (truths obscurely expressed,
maxims, and parables) of Solomon son of
David, king of Israel:
That people may know skillful and godly
Wisdom and instruction, discern and
comprehend the words of understanding
and insight*

Proverbs 1:1-2

The following scripture further depicts the relationship between wisdom and understanding. When you worship the Lord, your actions constitute wisdom. However, when you actually depart from sin, your actions demonstrate understanding.

*But to man He said, Behold, the reverential
and worshipful fear of the Lord—that*

is Wisdom; and to depart from evil is understanding.

Job 28:28

Millions have stood to worship God in a church service, singing praises and exalting His name. Some may even go to the altar to kneel at the Master's feet, showering Him with adoration. Starkly, only a fraction of those worshippers have departed from sin. The people without this understanding continue to do evil in the presence of God, deliberately and willingly, though God commands us to stay away from sin. The command consists of an understanding that must be marbled in our spirits as we seek after righteousness.

Instead of running after money, we should go after God, asking for His wisdom and understanding. If we're aiming directly at the money, we're reaching over wisdom and understanding. We have to go by way of wisdom and understanding, and with wisdom and understanding, money will follow.

My son, be attentive to my Wisdom [godly Wisdom learned by actual and costly experience], and incline your ear to my understanding [of what is becoming and prudent for you],

That you may exercise proper discrimination and discretion and your lips may guard and keep knowledge and the wise answer [to temptation].

Proverbs 5:1-2

Wisdom and understanding together also allow us to exercise discretion in our decisions and in what comes out of our mouths. When temptations come, we have to answer them with a response. Whenever we're tempted or the enemy says something to us, a conversation is initiated. The problem is that when that conversation arises, instead of talking right back to the problem, we let that situation do all the talking. Some will go to other people to complain, only repeating what the circumstance is dictating to them. Wisdom will tell you to go to God about each situation, but understanding is what will actually lead you to act upon any knowledge you receive.

Do you act according to your understanding in the Lord? Or, are you simply wise about what you should be doing? Many have the wisdom to know what's best for them, but they lack the understanding to act accordingly. This is why you see a lot of wise, stupid people who are in trouble.

For every circumstance that arises, use wisdom and understanding to give God's answer to temptation. The wisdom, or knowledge, is that a conversation starts whenever a situation arises. The understanding, or action, is that we have to talk back to that circumstance, allowing us to control it according to God's will.

God's Word is the understanding. So, if the enemy tries to strike you with discouragement, use a scripture in Psalms as your weapon. If the enemy tries to get you with fear, use a scripture that inspires courage to fight the battle. The key to applying understanding is to remember that each negative emotion should be treated like the spiritual warfare that it is. If you were in a physical war, you wouldn't hesitate to put on your armor. Likewise, you can't allow demonic emotions to sit and marinate in your mind. Immediately respond to them with the Word of truth that contradicts their lies.

Just as we can talk back to our situations, we can have also a conversation with wisdom.

> *Say to skillful and godly Wisdom, You are my sister, and regard understanding or insight as your intimate friend*
>
> Proverbs 7:4

In revisiting this verse, we find that wisdom and understanding are alive with personalities, they shouldn't be looked at as theories to be learned. We have to be sure within ourselves that we have a relationship with them, as if they were our sister or intimate friend. Their personified traits in the Bible beckon us to engage in a bond to share and to discover. To have a close relationship with wisdom and understanding, we should ask the Holy Spirit to teach us how to apply these spiritual benefits to our lives, continuously throughout each day.

Some people have great relationships with pity, or great relationships with guilt. They'll literally allow offense to cast a certain demeanor through their own bodies. They'll let pity control their minds. When we have a relationship with wisdom and understanding, we won't have a relationship with fear or doubt.

Don't tolerate relationships with the spirits that the devil sends. Have relationships with love, wisdom, mercy, kindness and forgiveness. Without understanding, negative spirits are quick to arise. When a difficult situation arises, fear is quick to come, along with its buddies: worry, stress, distrust and anger.

Heed to wisdom and abide by the Lord's understanding. Once you begin to commit and trust your works to God, you will see that your money, success and life will all begin to change for the better. You'll find a greater peace within yourself as you gain all that the Lord has for you. You'll also be ahead of many in the world who think that wisdom is all they need to get by. Now that you know better, you can explain to others that wisdom is not the only pertinent quality of a sound, Godly mind. Encourage your friends to not just know God's Word with wisdom, but to understand it so that they act in alignment with all the prosperity the Lord has for them. The blessings of God look good on us!

CHAPTER 15

THE ATTRACTIVENESS OF UNDERSTANDING

When we see people indulging in their sins, what are we offering them? What understanding from God can we give? When we demonstrate that we have understanding, people will be attracted to our insight and curious as to where the knowledge comes from. I remember a time in high school when I was talking to my teacher about God. In front of the whole class, I told her that she wouldn't be able to get to Heaven on the path that she was taking. As I was talking, a total hush came over the classroom. The students were all timidly looking at their desks, trying to avoid the awkward tension in the room.

The atmosphere of conviction was so heavy in our schoolroom that my teacher yelled out, "Shut up, Shane! You're scaring me." The class flinched.

"But it's the truth," I snapped back.

"I said, shut up!" she yelled back at me.

Seeing how people respond, often with a new reverence or sense of honor due to the understanding that you've imparted can be surprising. A few weeks later, that same teacher approached me and thanked me for sharing what God was saying on her behalf. God had convicted her to live for Him, and she was grateful. And even when those in the world don't agree with our Godly insight, they will often honor our lives because of the understanding that we choose to live by.

It's amazing how people will observe us when they know that we have understanding. When we have that attention on us, our behavior will certainly be judged by people—but the only judgment and opinion that we should be concerned about is God's. People will talk, but we only have to be mindful of how God perceives us.

Let's consider a man in the Bible named Joseph. Because of his amazing level of understanding, Pharaoh, the king of Egypt, put the young man in charge of the whole land.

> *And Pharaoh said to Joseph, Forasmuch as [your] God has shown you all this, there is nobody as intelligent and discreet and understanding and wise as you are.*
>
> *You shall have charge over my house, and all my people shall be governed according to your word [with reverence, submission, and obedience].*
>
> *Only in matters of the throne will I be greater than you are. Then Pharaoh said to Joseph, See, I have set you over all the land of Egypt.*
>
> Genesis 41:39-41

Pharaoh gave Joseph the privilege of ruling over all of Egypt because of what God had shown Joseph about Egypt. God gave Joseph a warning for Pharaoh about a coming famine and a solution for the horrifying dilemma. Pharaoh recognized and was attracted to the wonderful insight that Joseph had received from God.

I can imagine the conversation between Joseph and Pharaoh.

"Joseph, where did you get all of this knowledge about how to run a country? How did you know about the famine that would come for seven years?"

"God showed it to me. He gave me the understanding."

How many of us go into prayer to hear what God is saying and to receive His understanding so that others can be attracted to His understanding?

From Joseph's example, we can learn that understanding approves us for an appointment to a position. With the newfound insight from prayer, we are able to reach for positions that were previously unavailable to us. The position will fit perfectly with the understanding that God gives. For Joseph, his understanding elevated him to become a governor of Egypt.

When we hear what God is telling us, we act according to His Word. Others are instantly attracted, while God gets the glory. God wants to show us His vision and wants to build us up. We must diligently ask God, "Father, what are You saying? What are You showing me?"

People are not only attracted to understanding. They're also attracted to what understanding produces. What does understanding produce in our lives? In Deuteronomy 4, Moses gives instructions to the people of Israel and tells them the positive results that will come when they follow Moses' commands.

Now listen and give heed, O Israel, to the
statutes and ordinances which I teach you,
and do them, that you may live and go in

*and possess the land which the Lord, the
God of your fathers, gives you.*

*You shall not add to the word which I
command you, neither shall you diminish
it, that you may keep the commandments of
the Lord your God which I command you.*

Deuteronomy 4:1-2

*So keep them and do them, for that is your
wisdom and your understanding in the sight
of the peoples who, when they hear all these
statutes, will say, Surely this great nation is
a wise and understanding people.*

Deuteronomy 4:6

Moses told Israel to abide by the commandments of the Lord and that by their obeying God's Word, other nations would take notice. As the Israelites followed God's commandments, the other nations were attracted to the Israelite's obedience and the understanding that they received from God.

*For what great nation is there who has a god
so near to them as the Lord our God is to us
in all things for which we call upon Him?*

Deuteronomy 4:7

After observing the positive results of obeying God's understanding, the other nations would be astonished. They would ask, *Who is this God who gives understanding to His people and the people willingly and joyfully obey?* After all, their gods weren't alive. They prayed to bronze statues and animals that remained dormant and, well, dead.

> *He who is slow to anger has great understanding, but he who is hasty of spirit exposes and exalts his folly.*
>
> Proverbs 14:29

People are attracted to those who know how to stay calm. As I mentioned before, a person has great understanding if he is slow to anger. No one wants to be around a hothead. When something happens, he's ready to curse, ready to slap and ready to scratch. People don't like hanging around those who act as though they're upset with the world. A person of understanding will part with irritability because he knows that being quick to anger is not an attribute of God. He will become what the Bible considers to be *cool*.

> *He who has knowledge spares his words, and a man of understanding has a cool spirit.*
>
> Proverbs 17:27

The King James version translates a cool spirit into an excellent spirit, or a spirit of excellence. People are attracted to the excellence that people of great understanding display. Everything we do should be a glimmering example of our superior qualities in the Lord. Homework should be completed and neat. Projects at work should be turned in on time. Rooms should be kept clean.

Keep excellence around you at all times. Live it, speak it, act it and do it. Let people know if they're going to be around you, they're either going to be excellent or be on their way to becoming excellent. If we have people around us who don't strive to abide by the excellence that comes with understanding, we will ultimately lose the attractiveness that God has given us.

When we're unsure how to choose our friends and associates, the book of Proverbs let's us know that we must rely on the strength of God's understanding to surround us with wise men and women.

> *Discretion shall watch over you, understanding shall keep you,*
> *To deliver you from the way of evil and the evil men, from men who speak perverse things and are liars,*
> *Men who forsake the paths of uprightness to walk in the ways of darkness,*
> *Who rejoice to do evil and delight in the perverseness of evil,*
> *Who are crooked in their ways, wayward and devious in their paths.*
>
> Proverbs 2:11-15

Understanding ensures that we are separated from people who participate in evil activities, people who are liars and people who aren't on the path of righteousness. The separation leaves room for those who are respectable company to keep.

Understanding causes God's people to be attractive. If we seek God for understanding, people will notice, as God does things so amazing that we are humbled by His mercy. A key to keeping this attractiveness is to ensure that we're careful about those we deem as friends. While the prosperity that comes with God's understanding will be compelling to all, it's our responsibility to manage well our Godly assets.

Living in this world, I have witnessed that losing our blessings is so much easier than obtaining them. Everyone who notices your charismatic qualities does not have your best interest at heart. The Lord is open to all, and those who *choose* to not embrace His love are not the friends we need to keep. Be careful who you allow to enter your sphere. Don't let people bring negative influences into your life that will replace the understanding God has given you.

CHAPTER 16
UNDERSTANDING REPLACES

Often, we find ourselves crying out to God because we've replaced His original intentions with our own will. He hears those cries and is present to help us. Over and over again, He becomes the thread that binds together a torn situation. Although He comes to the rescue, we lose valuable chances to grow in faith each time we step out on our own understanding. How powerful would our lives be if we didn't act in a way counter to God's will just because we didn't understand? If we would only learn to trust Him, He wouldn't have to fix what He told us to stay away from. He wouldn't have to repair the negatives that result from our doubt in Him.

When we become too focused on worldly standards to recognize the potential depth of a grave situation, we run the risk of finding comfort in something God has warned us to reject. As our Dad and Protector, God wants to replace the negative in our lives with endless positives. Unfortunately, He's unable to because we're not sufficiently disappointed with the negatives.

We will never seek a replacement if we're not frustrated with what is already there. The sex we have outside the bond of marriage, the ungodly relationships we maintain and the greed we allow to consume us may feel good for a moment's time, but the havoc we create from disobeying God is *never* worth the sin. The satisfaction we feel from sin is what Satan uses to deceive us.

We know that stepping out against God's commandments will hurt us but we tend to ignore our consciences. In fear of disappointing others, we disappoint God and grow to find contentment because the people around us are happy with our actions. "This is just how I am," we tell ourselves. All along, we're completely unaware that our disobedience will place us in a chaotic situation that God never intended for us.

If we know that what we have in our lives is inadequate and if we believe that God has better for us, then we'll have a hunger for God to replace our lack with His abundance. If we can allow Him to do this, then we'll be able to let His changes work for our benefit. The Bible gives us clear instructions as to how we can use God's insight to replace our unwholesome traits. Ridding ourselves of these elements isn't enough, though. We have to replace the space with God's understanding. Otherwise, the negatives will be gone, but the harm may return.

> *Teach me, and I will hold my peace; and*
> *cause me to understand wherein I have erred.*
>
> Job 6:24

Many of us have erred. As humans, it's inevitable that we will slip up sometimes. The key to lessening our mistakes is to seek the Lord *before* we act. If we include God in even the smallest of our decisions, we won't have to worry about larger issues developing later on.

God desires to correct our wrongdoings more than we want Him to, but the more we run away from His desire to correct our errors, the more we leave for Him to replace later with His understanding. It's one thing to say that we're unaware of the best solution to a problem, but it's another to deliberately disregard what we know we should be doing. Many people haven't had parents to teach them right from wrong. Others are ignorant because they purposefully choose to neglect the caring instructions that have been allotted to them. In either case, ignorance always causes errors, which later requires God's replacement of understanding for the negatives in someone's life.

> *He takes away understanding from the leaders of the people of the land and of the earth, and causes them to wander in a wilderness where there is no path.*
>
> Job 12:24

The further removed we are from God's understanding, the closer we find ourselves to mistakes and disorientation. When God's understanding is absent, we stumble about aimlessly. From today's viewpoint, the scripture above can refer to people in life who don't know what they are doing, what path they're taking or what goals they should pursue. They haven't allowed God's understanding to replace their confusion, causing them to be confused about what's going on in their lives or how to proceed. Instead of seeking the Lord before their goals end in failure, they move on to their next endeavor, without any consideration for God's opinion. They spend their entire lives feeling lost, wondering why something seems to be missing.

People who are spiritually at a loss make statements such as, "Nothing is going right for me, so I'm going to kill myself." In their bewilderment, they come to drastic conclusions to match the delusions created in their minds. Because they are pursuing worldly goals rather than a Godly relationship, they're sensitive to evil thoughts, and become easily susceptible to making irrational decisions.

People who are mentally disoriented have lost their bearings. They've managed to wander throughout life in an unstable and unbalanced fashion. While God wants to replace our incomprehension with His insight, He can only do so if we permit Him to. When we let our own will take control of our lives, our pursuits lack purpose. Using understanding as a replacement for confusion allows us to stay focused and on the right track, both spiritually and mentally.

> *With the aged [you say] is wisdom, and*
> *with length of days comes understanding.*
> *But [only] with [God] are [perfect] wisdom*
> *and might; He [alone] has [true] counsel and*
> *understanding.*
>
> Job 12:12-13

Once we've searched for and sought the Lord, finally receiving his direction and understanding, a strong temptation arises. Somehow, we become persuaded to rely on our own reasoning instead of following God's path for us. As the dialogues of Job note, true understanding only comes from God, not from our own intellect.

Understanding replaces reason. Feelings are the voice of the body. Reason is the voice of the mind. Conscience is the voice of the human spirit. Reason is the mind's voice trying to mold concepts into solutions that makes sense for that person. When the mind is hard at work trying to reason, we'll hear phrases like, "I know what God said, but I can't really see that happening."

Trying to figure things out is synonymous with leaning to our own understanding. Against all reason, God's insight should be the ultimate authority in our lives. In the Bible, we find a blind man who cried out to Jesus for healing. Jesus abandoned all logic, rubbed mud on the blind man's eyes and told him to wash in the pool of Siloam, a place used for ceremonial cleansing before entering the Temple area. Despite all *reason*, the blind man received his sight by being obedient to Jesus. Reason says a person can't receive his sight by putting mud on his eyes and performing an act of cleansing, but understanding takes the Word of God and puts it into action, abandoning all thought. Let's replace reason with understanding.

> But I have understanding as well as you; I am not inferior to you. Who does not know such things as these [of God's wisdom and might]?
>
> Job 12:3

If we have low self-esteem, even if it's only in certain areas, we have a gap in our understanding. Areas of low self-esteem, often masked as humility, are the parts of our lives that we need to replace with God's understanding. Instead of marking ourselves inferior to our neighbor, we must use God's understanding to know who we are in Christ.

Although God has instructed us to teach others, we allow our mental blocks to hinder us from fulfilling His plans. Often, we believe that we don't have the looks, brains or status to teach one another. As the book of Job hints, we should have no form of inferiority complex.

> *What do you know that we know not? What do you understand that is not equally clear to us?*
>
> Job 15:9

Understanding replaces whatever is unclear. If something is unclear to us, we have to get the understanding. Reading that last sentence, we nod our heads, thinking, *of course!* But to some people, this isn't common knowledge. If they hear something that they don't understand, they'll say: "I don't understand," or "I don't know," instead of going after the understanding.

Don't be too shy to ask questions. The person who asks the majority of the questions in class is often the one who will eventually understand the most. Success isn't just about attaining a certain stature, it's about the level of understanding you have regarding a certain topic. So, if you're unclear about something, ask. If others laugh, ignore them.

Don't be ashamed to seek God's understanding to replace any lack of clarity in your life. Whether the area you're uncertain about is a job, a car, a change of location, a relationship or a friend, never hesitate to say to the Lord, "Father, I'm unclear. Replace my thoughts with Your insight. Make Your understanding clear to me. I want to follow Your divine path for my life." God will be pleased with your pursuit. A request for the understanding and clarity *you need* will always be answered.

Be hungry for God's insights to replace your thoughts about every aspect of your life. This chapter outlines only a mere fraction of what understanding can replace. Errors, disorientation, reason, low self-esteem and lack of clarity are just a few of the many areas God desires to make easier for us. His grace is abundant and waiting to set you free from the locking grip of Satan, who tries to keep you captive.

Let God do the work of replacing the negative with His positive as you grow stronger in faith. His instructions are always clear, and if we properly seek His advice, they're given to us *before* we head in the wrong direction. Seeking those instructions and abiding by them are the characteristics of a great student of God's understanding. If all we did was simply obey, according to the understanding He has given us, He would have nothing to replace, because righteousness would be our only possession.

CHAPTER 17
THE STUDENTS OF UNDERSTANDING

Surely I am more brutish than any man,
and have not the understanding of a man.
I neither learned wisdom, nor have the
knowledge of the holy.

Proverbs 30:2-3, KJV

If we don't know God, what do we really know? Being students of God's understanding should be a top priority in our lives. Our academic and work accolades won't mean anything when we stand before Jesus Christ. Chasing after money and career are trivial pursuits in contrast to the love and peace of our Father. The wisdom and understanding that we get from God supersedes any secular knowledge that we glean from the world around us.

The path to being students of understanding starts with our Bible reading habits. A personal Bible study before the Lord is essential to our growth. We can't simply rely on the lessons that preachers present on Sunday to get us through the week. Like any relationship, our standing with God can only become stronger once we decide to put in personal time with Him.

I've found that the best way to read the Bible isn't the method of reading chapter after chapter. Each day, we can read a few verses of scripture and meditate on it throughout the day. As we take those scriptures with us, and allow them to seep into our hearts, we will find ourselves becoming learners of Scripture while also becoming better at living God's most holy Word.

We will find it advantageous when we read parts of the Bible that correlate to an area of our lives of current, even pressing, interest so that we can directly apply those scriptures to what we're going through. If someone is dealing with being too quick to anger, my recommendation would be to research scriptures on that topic. If you're struggling with forgiveness, ponder on verses that point to such. Include the scriptures that relate to your situation as a part of your daily, continual walk with God, and allow what you've read to be the understanding that your life requires.

We shouldn't be the masters of our personal time with God, taking over the flow of the moment without any care for His concerns. Those special times with Him should be a conversation between you and God, not a speech from you. Wait and be patient for God to answer your requests. When you get Him to say something concerning your situation, you can rest assured He'll stand behind His Word.

Also, be sure that your prayer time includes moments where you simply enjoy God's presence. How much would you want to hang out with a friend if your time together only included you being bombarded with questions? Sometimes, the Lord wants us to be honest about our needs, and other times He just wants us to enjoy His company. Great students of the Lord understand the importance of basking in God's peaceful presence in humility, without inquiries. Learn His voice to understand which direction He wants to take you in prayer. Allow His Holy Spirit to lead you.

In prayer, don't forget that blessings and gifts are attached to understanding. The Lord can't release certain gifts until the receiver has the understanding to properly manage them. The spiritual realm contains infinite numbers of blessings, waiting for people to understand them before God can allow their glory to be manifested here on Earth. The more we dive into God's Word, the more we can understand who He is. "I am that I am," He has told us. We can never say we know enough about Him. The person who stops learning, stops growing. The person who stops growing, stops living. In the manner of the attentive student in the classroom who can never get enough of the subject, make sure that your life is abundant with God's understanding and get all of it that you can.

Like the young men in the tribe of Judah, when we receive understanding from God, we will be elevated to higher places. These four young men were favored by the King of Babylon, Nebuchadnezzar, because of their relationship with God and the understanding that they received from the Lord.

> *As for these four youths, God gave them knowledge and skill in all learning and wisdom, and Daniel had understanding in all [kinds of] visions and dreams.*
>
> *Now at the end of the time which the king had set for bringing [all the young men in], the chief of the eunuchs brought them before Nebuchadnezzar.*
>
> *And the king conversed with them, and among them all none was found like Daniel,*

*Hananiah, Mishael, and Azariah; therefore
they were assigned to stand before the king.*

*And in all matters of wisdom and
understanding concerning which the king
asked them, he found them ten times
better than all the [learned] magicians and
enchanters who were in his whole realm.*

Daniel 1:17-20

These four young men loved God's understanding and
were students of His insight. They constantly gleaned what
God was saying about every circumstance, and it showed. The
king recognized that the youths' understanding was not only
excellent, but better than those with worldly wisdom.

You too can be honored on this level by standing before God.
If you want to go back to school but God is telling you to wait,
then be patient. If you want to get a promotion but God is telling
you "not yet," then hold off. God uses our seasons of patience
to train and mold us to understand life from His perspective.
If you can learn to be humble in waiting, God will reveal your
talents at the proper time. When it is that time, people will
definitely notice the difference in you, and like the young men
of Judah, you will be recognized. The honor you receive from
learning to trust God's understanding will be greater than any
acknowledgment attained in a worldly manner.

When you do get to the season when God is ready to
showcase your understanding, you may run into a situation
where He desires you to share what you have learned. While
sharing, make sure that you're teaching in a respectful way.
Don't be condescending to those who may know less than you
do. Remember that at one point we all knew less than those

around us. Having a loving, pleasant manner will allow God to use you best.

> *The wise in heart are called prudent, understanding, and knowing, and winsome speech increases learning [in both speaker and listener].*
>
> Proverbs 16:21

The scripture above says that winsome, or attractive, speech increases learning. When understanding is taught, it has to be done in an appealing manner. Many people in the world don't understand the need for God. We have to prove to others that God's understanding is worth having, but we can only do so by teaching with love. In advertising, dozens of commercials use sexuality because that's what seems to appeal to the world. When we demonstrate the goodness of God's knowledge, we have to appeal to others using God's most attractive characteristic: love.

Sometimes you may find yourself teaching God's understanding and other times you may be the one who acts as the recipient. Since everyone learns differently, receiving God's understanding through those around us can now and then seem to be a challenging path. Regardless of whether you are the student or the giver, remember that we all gain understanding by way of different coaching methods.

While some may have learning styles that are straightforward, others may require a less direct form of teaching. The more aligned the instruction is with the student's learning style, the more attractive the message will be to the student. For example, I know that some members of my congregation are less receptive to being corrected than others. I don't judge them for their differences because I simply know that different personalities require different forms of teaching.

If the Holy Spirit leads me to correct members who are easily offended, I may decide to instruct in a joking manner. That way, they don't feel as if they're being criticized. This method causes them to let down their wall of pride and open themselves to be more receptive to the message.

For the members who humbly open their hearts for correction, a joke is not necessary to get the point across. I can be firmer with them because I know they'll receive the correction in the spirit in which I intended it.

Whichever way God desires to deliver the message to us, we must be very careful to listen to it. We can't simply regard God's Word as thoughts proceeding from the perspective of a human heart only because a person is the one delivering the message. The person teaching may well be serving as God's mouthpiece, and in such a case, the communication isn't coming from the person talking. The lesson may actually be coming from the Lord, using the individual. We have to remember, this is the *Creator* of the universe, Who cares enough to correct us. God's words aren't just advice. They are orders, and His understanding is the command. After receiving such a correction, of course, seek God's direct input on the matter at hand.

> *Your hands have made me, cunningly fashioned and established me; give me understanding, that I may learn Your commandments.*
>
> Psalm 119:73

When God commands, we need to understand His directions. Ask the Lord, *Why do You want me to do what You have commanded? What is the purpose?* By asking these questions, we're not trying to discredit the commandment. Rather, we want the command to be so much ingrained in us that it becomes a part of our being. Sometimes, God may immediately reply to our questions. Other times, He may choose to wait to give us further information. Either way, trust His instructions and obey with faith.

There is a difference between following God out of obligation versus obeying Him out of pure love. We have to get to a point in our relationship where we don't follow God's commands simply because we should, but because we want to. We need to be hungry for Him to instruct our day. Let's not focus on a personal schedule, but keep our minds on what God is commanding us to do for that day. Then, we must be open to take the path He's leading us on.

Those who are open to deviating from their own intentions in order to carry out God's plans are those who have His understanding. Being led by the Lord will often require us to go outside of our comfort zones. If we always stayed in a static, complacent mindset, we could never watch ourselves grow. We have to be open to changing our ways, even if it means becoming accustomed to an understanding, a way of seeing, that we were once unfamiliar with. Those who understand more, increase in knowledge. Those who increase in knowledge, elevate.

> *Strike a scoffer, and the simple will learn prudence; reprove a man of understanding, and he will increase in knowledge.*
>
> Proverbs 19:25

Being receptive to God's correction is one of the most authentic ways that we can be open to His insight. It shows God that we trust Him and that we're willing to die to our ways to learn more about His. When we do this, we begin to transform in our character and our behavior.

Learning about God and His wisdom is a continuous process. We can do this by making sure that the Lord is included in every decision of our lives, whether it's as large a matter as getting a new car or as small as purchasing an outfit. Saying that we must ask God about everything may sound extreme, but that's the kind of relationship He wants with us. He wants to be included in *all* aspects of our lives, no matter how minor we may perceive those aspects to be.

The importance of seeking God's input in everything isn't really about the outcome of each step we take or each choice we might consider making. No. But if we've already trained ourselves to hear His voice daily, we're always prepared to hear His commands when trouble reveals itself. The more we open up to Him about the small cares, the easier it is to hear His voice about the larger issues.

Let's aim to do all that God asks of us. Let's not be average for Him, but be superb. Let's be the students who attend to God in every matter. Having a relationship with the Lord is not just about worshipping Him on Sunday, it's about making Him a part of our lives on the deepest level. Let's always remember that the greatest students don't just attend their classes at the appointed time, they are continuously applying the subject matter to their lives, even long after the semester ends. Being consistent requires a huge payment in attention, time and energy, but the rewards are well worth the effort.

CHAPTER 18
COSTS OF UNDERSTANDING

I remember hearing a certain old Gospel song as a child that went: "The same thing it took to get salvation, it's gonna take the same thing to keep it." It takes heavy doses of humbleness, meekness and surrender to get salvation and it takes the same attributes to stay open to God's Word.

Understanding works just like salvation—we pay a price to maintain it. The cost is to yield ourselves through obedience and sacrifice. To gain God's insight, we have to deny our own way of thinking and cling to His understanding. Denial of the self is the sacrifice we must make to sustain a relationship with the Lord. It's the price we pay if we value God's understanding in our lives.

Through Christ, we are able to understand even our most troublesome of circumstances. We have a remarkable opportunity to harvest huge benefits from knowing how to understand, but unless we're willing to pay the price, these benefits will never be reaped by us. Having to abandon our selfish desires is not one of the costs of understanding for no reason—it's the way the process works for our best outcomes. The gift of understanding gives us knowledge of what to do about a situation, but the sacrificial acts we commit to are what teach us to obey God's will over our own.

If God were to give us all the understanding we desire without teaching us how to sacrifice, we would never put His understanding into use because we would only be accustomed to living our lives out of our own will. We would have His understanding, but not be obedient to its requirements.

We must admit that we need understanding, regardless of whether attaining it requires sacrifice as the cost. Some people may say, "I want a better relationship with God, but I've just been too busy with work and friends." The prideful idea of pretending to be in need of nothing, causes us to miss out on what God has in store for us. We can't be oblivious to our need for God simply because we aren't ready to sacrifice the time. We give up time for everything else, so why not for God also?

God has an abundant supply ready to meet each and every one of our needs. He wants to supply all our desires, but we have to be willing to sacrifice for Him to do so. Anything God asks of us is always worth forfeiting for the sake of His will being carried out in our lives.

> Give me understanding, that I may keep
> Your law; yes, I will observe it with my whole
> heart.
>
> Psalm 119:34

We have to understand that we can receive no greater reward than the ability to feel the love of God. We are very familiar with the prosperity and comfort of the world; however, we must remember that our sacrifices for God are of more value than worldly pursuits. The sacrifices we make for the Lord will always be given back to us in abundance, while the sacrifices made in the world will only be counted as a loss. We see those who are wealthy becoming wealthier and more at ease with being Godless each day. On the other hand, we observe those who serve God faithfully, yet they struggle financially. The psalmist of the following verses was tempted to speak out negatively concerning the apparent disparity.

> *Behold, these are the ungodly, who always prosper and are at ease in the world; they increase in riches.*
>
> *Surely then in vain have I cleansed my heart and washed my hands in innocency.*
>
> *For all the day long have I been smitten and plagued, and chastened every morning.*
>
> *Had I spoken thus [and given expression to my feelings], I would have been untrue and have dealt treacherously against the generation of Your children.*
>
> *But when I considered how to understand this, it was too great an effort for me and too painful*
>
> *Until I went into the sanctuary of God; then I understood [for I considered] their end.*
>
> Psalm 73:12-17

The psalmist's cry was answered in prayer. He received the understanding that even though the wicked seemed to be more prosperous than God's servants, they would ultimately end in misery and ruin, causing a life of sacrifice unto God to be more attractive and desirable.

Unwilling to obey the Lord, the ungodly purposefully chose paths that aligned with their own understanding, not God's. They sought after the desires of their heart ahead of getting God's understanding. When the time came that God instructed them to let go of their possessions for their own good, they refused to sacrifice because they valued their treasures more than God's insight.

As you read the following psalmist's testimony of praise unto God, you will discover the certainty of the tragic end of the ungodly:

> How great are Your doings, O Lord! Your thoughts are very deep.
> A man in his rude and uncultivated state knows not, neither does a [self-confident] fool understand this:
> That though the wicked spring up like grass and all evildoers flourish, they are doomed to be destroyed forever.
>
> Psalm 92:5-7

In addition to their being unwilling to make sacrifices, the other matter that keeps people from understanding is that they simply refuse to ask. They would easily be able to escape a life of destruction if they were just obedient to the pull that God places on them. Time after time, the Lord tugs on the hearts of the ungodly, hoping they will choose Him, yet they continuously reject His call. Blind to their own destruction, they see no need to ask for the Lord's insight. The scripture below plainly shows how practical it is to make this request.

> *Your hands have made me, cunningly fashioned and established me; give me understanding, that I may learn Your commandments.*
>
> Psalm 119:73

Once we have expressed our desire for understanding *and* we believe we have received what we've requested, our insight into life becomes much clearer. We gain clarity because the understanding we've obtained from the Lord empowers our spiritual eyes to pierce the depths of His knowledge. As this next scripture declares, faithful meditation will help us to understand our lives even further.

> *I have better understanding and deeper insight than all my teachers, because Your testimonies are my meditation.*
>
> Psalm 119:99

Obedience to God's instructions and meditation on His Word are what place us in a position to receive God's mighty understanding. Sometimes, though, God may not speak a Word to us directly. Instead, He will command us to listen to one of our elders, brothers, or sisters. Common sense should motivate us to listen to those whom God tells us to hear, but our own ideologies and experiences have convinced us that we sometimes can afford to disobey. Putting aside our own beliefs for the respect of God's requests demonstrates a sacrifice. When we reject the opportunity to make such a sacrifice, we limit our ability to acquire an understanding that God could be trying to deliver to us through someone else.

> *The reverent fear and worship of the Lord is the beginning of Wisdom and skill [the preceding and the first essential, the prerequisite and the alphabet]; a good understanding, wisdom, and meaning have all those who do [the will of the Lord]. Their praise of Him endures forever.*
>
> Psalm 111:10

Like anything else in this world, receiving understanding exacts a price. While sacrificing our will to act in obedience to the Lord may seem daunting, it's much better than going along our own path, courting peril. The ways of a man will always seem wise in his own eyes, but he doesn't realize that those pursuits will end in spiritual death. The cost of sacrificing is worth the rewards of receiving true Godly insight.

Many in the world will make their own selfish sacrifices, quickly rising up the ladder of worldly success. While watching these people succeed in their evil may be perplexing, we must remember that any success attained without Godly sacrifice will only end in ruin.

Trusting God in your obedience to Him is important. Don't obey God while lacking faith in His promises. If He says that He will do something, know that He will. The sacrifices you make to live a Godly life will never be in vain, especially when you open your heart to give understanding to someone who needs it.

CHAPTER 19
GIVING UNDERSTANDING

The lips of the [uncompromisingly] righteous
feed and guide many, but fools die for want
of understanding and heart.

Proverbs 10:21

There are those right now who will die without ever having understood their purpose on this Earth. They don't have God's understanding, and even worse, they don't have anyone who's willing to give it to them. The scripture above tells us that these people need help. Yet, minding our own business has become our custom.

We know that others have many problems. Unfortunately, we keep our heads down as if we don't see them. "I wish I could help but I have so many things on my plate right now," we tell ourselves. Knowing that God can use the smallest moment of assistance as an opportunity to minister is critical. When others are misguided, our duty is to show them the way.

Sharing God's insight with others should be what we want to do. Often, we know the understanding that ought to be given, but doubt keeps us from offering our knowledge. We should hunger to give the love of God to those in need.

The reason why we shy away from helping others is because of the devil. The devil knows that God's understanding will help people to better themselves in the Lord. So, instead of allowing us to share our knowledge, he says to us, "Who are you to tell them about themselves?" or "They'll get mad at you if you tell them that." The deceitful, persuasive thoughts he puts in our heads are simply a ploy to keep us from sharing the truth.

Many times, the devil will keep us from helping someone, but he'll convince us to talk about that person. Talking about what someone *should* do shows we know what they need to do. So, if we can talk about someone, then we can *help* them.

As Christians, we are only a little lower than the angels (Hebrews 2:6-8), as the Bible teaches us. We have more power than the devil, so all that's left to do is to use it. People won't recognize the God in us until we show them our actions through His heart. When we share our understanding, people can see the light in us for themselves. Through Christ, we do have power, and we are the light of the world. Don't believe anything different.

So many are suffering from a lack of understanding. They don't understand their lives, their goals, their choices or their actions. They're too embarrassed to ask for help, so they walk around feeling lost. Some of them are even suicidal. Giving understanding can prevent someone from doing harm to themselves or to others.

Look at all the bombings, killings and school shootings in today's world. They *all* could have been prevented had someone given those people understanding. Before the guns were in their hands, someone could have told them that they were good enough, smart enough and important enough to succeed in Christ. God wants *all* of His children to know the best about themselves, but He can't hop off His throne to help them. That's why He's left us His Holy Spirit. The ability to encourage is in *us*. Because the Lord loves His people, He's sending us to be the answer to the world. We are the answer, and God is trying to connect answers to problems every day.

In many instances, what prevents us from giving understanding is that we don't want people to be mad at us. Putting that on the scale next to what could happen if we don't give understanding, the matter that could be avoided becomes weightier. I believe that we would rather have people angry at us than for them to injure themselves, ruin their marriages or watch their families fall apart.

God's instructions to share understanding are no different for those whom we dislike. Out of the billions of people on this Earth, He has chosen **us** to be the helpers. Regardless of whether individuals have done us wrong, it's *still* our responsibility to help them when they're in need. Prayer isn't an excuse to hinder ourselves from helping those in need. We can't say, "I'll pray for them," when God has already blessed us to be the answer to the prayer. Often, someone has already been praying for the betterment of that person and *we* are the result of that prayer.

God doesn't care whether we're on perfect terms with the party He desires us to speak to. He calls us to minister to His people regardless of any hurt we may have felt. Forgiveness must take place on contact. So, even if the pain is still on our hearts, the grudge should be in God's hands. If that pain causes us to dislike someone, God *still* calls us to love the individual. Sharing God's understanding is certainly a part of that love.

Not only is sharing understanding an action of love, but it's also an act of peace. When we share understanding, not only do we impart peace into a once confusing situation, but we also allow others to take steps toward positive change. When we think about God's love, we can remember where we were before accepting Christ. As we ponder those moments, thinking about how far salvation has brought us is amazing.

Through His love, we're no longer ignorant, but we have knowledge. We have an understanding of the best choices, the best paths and the best actions we can provide ourselves. His understanding is no different. The impartation of it literally causes us to move from one place to the other, guiding us on the right track and putting peace in our hearts. Realizing this, why would we ever want to deny those who are suffering that kind of momentum to finally move out of their negative circumstances?

When we don't share our understanding, we intentionally keep others from experiencing God's love through a change in their situation. God often works through changes. How can others experience those transformations until we give them the understanding of what to do? We have to allow peace to develop in every wrong that we see.

Peace is not the calm, tranquil feeling that comes after all of the turmoil has left. Peace is the force that tears through the confusion, sets situations in order and brings order to chaos. God's peace brings law to the lawless and commands worry and fear to depart. The result of peace is serenity of mind and its surroundings. If God is telling us to be the forceful movement of peaceful change, then go forth and do what He asks of you without hesitation.

In the Bible, Joseph's actions were certainly an example of a powerful, peace-bringing transformation. More importantly, he didn't hesitate to share the insight that God had given him. God used Joseph to impart an understanding that elevated him from being a slave to acting as the governor over one of the most powerful nations on Earth.

His rise came from a small opportunity to give understanding to Pharaoh's butler and chef. Both the chef and the butler had dreams that only Joseph could understand. Joseph was able to get the insight from God to give interpretations of the dreams. Two years later, when Pharaoh himself had a confusing dream, Joseph was called upon for help.

Joseph told Pharaoh that the dream meant that the entire land of Egypt would suffer from a seven-year famine and that the land needed to store and ration its produce. After hearing Joseph's words, Pharaoh was astounded:

> *And Pharaoh said to Joseph, Forasmuch as [your] God has shown you all this, there is nobody as intelligent and discreet and understanding and wise as you are.*
>
> Genesis 41:39

The understanding that Joseph gave to Pharaoh literally saved entire nations from starving. Out of all the intellectuals of Egypt, Pharaoh chose Joseph for wise counsel because of his courage to share the understanding that God had given him for others. What understanding is God giving us to give to His people? Are we taking advantage of every opportunity to share what God has given us?

Understanding is a wellspring of life to those who have it, but to give instruction to fools is folly.

Proverbs 16:22

Pharaoh was extremely receptive to the knowledge that Joseph was willing to share with him. Unfortunately, this may not always be the case regarding the people whom we share God's insight with. In my years of pastoring and sharing the Word of God with those around me, I have found that some are eager to hear what I have to say, while others are less excited to be around the understanding that I'm trying to give them.

As the scripture above says, many fools reside in the world, and giving instructions to them is folly, or foolish. These people have no desire to know God or to change their lives. Many of them are fully aware that they're intentionally running from the Lord. No matter what we do, they'll reject God's understanding. If we come up against a situation like this, we should know that their negative reaction is not our fault.

We are to share the message of Christ and understanding with *all* whom the Holy Spirit leads us to. We can only control ourselves in doing what God leads us to do. We can't control how others react to our obedience. Once we're able to recognize a person's foolish character, however, we know to not keep sharing those same instructions with them, over and over again.

If I have a friend who constantly shows up late to work, God may lead me to tell her that her poor work habits will negatively affect her overall performance. If that friend continuously shows up late, despite what the Lord has led me to tell her, I now know that she is a fool. I'm not going to keep giving her the same advice. If I do that, then I become the one engaging in folly.

Be open to sharing the insight of the Lord with everyone, regardless of whether the message is received in the manner we intend for it to be. We must act in a Christ-like fashion as we share God's love with others. God doesn't just share His insight because He *should*; He does it because He *wants* to. Don't just think of sharing understanding as your duty. Make it your desire to see everyone else experience success in their personal lives.

CHAPTER 20
SUCCESS FROM UNDERSTANDING

Seeking God brings us the success we *need* instead of the success that we desire. Many of us scramble to achieve in certain endeavors, but we fail each time, not knowing that God is actually trying to protect us from a path that we only *think* we want, but really don't.

It's often said that people in actual fact don't know what they want. Following our own understanding of success may lead us to our desires, but not necessarily to our fulfillment. This is why many times in life we work hard for something, then months later we find ourselves saying, "Hmm...is this really what I want?"

Real fulfillment can only derive from God. He is our Creator, and a true relationship with Him is where prosperity lies. Why do you think many of the most affluent people in the world commit suicide? They may have money, but they don't feel fulfilled. Even if we have money, cars and clothes, we don't have true success until God grants it to us. Having His understanding is a great part of having success in Him.

Many people seek success and fail because they don't realize that success isn't what should be sought. Others attain what they were hoping for, but quickly lose it because they don't have the understanding to maintain it. If you seek after your purpose by living for God, He will be the One to grant you exactly what you need to be successful. Even more important, you'll be able to hold onto the success because you have the understanding to keep what you've worked so hard for.

> *And beware lest you say in your [mind and] heart, My power and the might of my hand have gotten me this wealth.*
>
> *But you shall [earnestly] remember the Lord your God, for it is He Who gives you power to get wealth, that He may establish His covenant which He swore to your fathers, as it is this day.*
>
> Deuteronomy 8:17-18

As the scripture above tells us, God is the Source of all people's wealth. It is He Who controls the actions of others and the money on this Earth. No matter what someone has, he can't give it to you unless God allows him to. Nothing is wrong with networking toward success, but your focus should be on the Lord, not on the others around you. Don't seek people and hope that people will bless you. Seek God and allow Him to bless you through people.

We should never make the attaining of wealth and titles our goal. Doing this can cause us to lose sight of completing our purpose on the Earth. We must seek God for His understanding, not positions or finances. Money and positions will always follow the one who has the understanding to maintain them. When you have understanding, God can trust you to manage what He has for you.

For you say, I am rich; I have prospered and grown wealthy, and I am in need of nothing; and you do not realize and understand that you are wretched, pitiable, poor, blind, and naked.

Revelation 3:17

Success is understanding's primary benefit, but God's view of success is different from the world's. With God, it's not about the number of dollars He allows us to have. He's already given us the greatest love there is, His Son.

Once we have accepted Jesus and continuously follow the lead of the Holy Spirit, we're well on our way to having true success, which occurs once we have fulfilled our life's purpose on the Earth. If we want success, all we have to do is live according to what He tells us to do by abiding in righteous character.

Imagine if everyone only had a secular view of success. The entire world would be a selfish place to live in. It's a blessing that some people still define success according to God's understanding of love.

When I was a little boy a gentleman lived across the street from my grandmother whom we called "Mr. RB." Mr. RB was one of those people who understood success from God's point of view.

One day, my grandmother needed some work done, and Mr. RB had the expertise for the task. It took him hours to repair the appliance.

After he corrected the problem, my grandmother asked, "What do I owe you?"

I will never forget his answer. He said, "Nothing but a smile."

I could tell that his response shocked my grandmother because, totally unlike her, she was speechless. She just stood there staring at him with her eyes stretched. She looked a bit confused, but his words made her smile. They embraced briefly, and she said, "Thank you so very much..." as he walked back across the street to his home.

Isn't it nice that some people can appreciate a smile as payment enough for the work they've done? Mr. RB's understanding of success was being able to help the people he loved.

> *This Book of the Law shall not depart out of your mouth, but you shall meditate on it day and night, that you may observe and do according to all that is written in it. For then you shall make your way prosperous, and then you shall deal wisely and have good success.*
>
> Joshua 1:8

According to the scripture above, success is dependent on the meditation on God's Word. Meditation on the Word will also provide us with the ability to maintain our success because of the knowledge we attain from its sound instructions. If we follow the words that we read, we will find that God's wisdom can easily make our business dealings, company relationships and family lives all operate more efficiently.

The wisdom allotted from the Word of God is unlike any other wisdom in the world. So, if we can trust the path of God's success, we will surely see ourselves prospering further than those who conduct business the worldly way. Not only will we have prosperity, but the success He blesses us with will accompany His grace, protection and peace of mind. Also, we will have a relationship with the Creator of the universe who will have the ability to say He trusts our methods.

As Christians, we know our positions of success are synonymous with our comprehension of the Word of God. As our understanding of God's Word increases, so do our blessings and our levels of success. God is always ready to bless all of His people, He just needs our obedience to do so. Once He has that, the blessings automatically overflow in abundance, not in our time, but in His.

Once the Bible is an incorporated part of our lives, the steps that we take will be in the direction where God will be able to bless us. We'll be in the right place at the right time to receive what He has been waiting to give. All that will be left to do is for us to have patience. The more that we're able to put God's Word into practice, the more God will have His hand in every situation. As with any state of affairs, we shouldn't seek God's Word simply to improve the likelihood of our success. We must be sure that our motives are always governed by God's understanding, to do as He would have us do, and all the good that the Lord has for us will follow.

A CALL FROM THE ALTAR

Our Father, all those who have read this book, I bring them and their needs before You now. You are Jehovah Jireh, our Provider. We expect from You, by faith, knowing that You will meet our needs according to Your riches in the very glory of Your presence.

My Lord Jesus, said, "All that the Father giveth me shall come to me; and him that cometh to me I will in no wise cast out." (John 6:37)

Dear Father, as these who have read Understanding bring You their praise, prayer and supplication, I know you will answer them according to Your most holy, just and righteous will.

All these things I ask and pray in the name of my Lord and Savior, Jesus Christ! Father, because I know that You will answer my prayer, I thank You in the name of Jesus Christ!

Oh Lord our God, for all of these and other blessings: we glorify, honor, praise, thank, bless, worship, adore, extol, exalt, magnify and celebrate YOU in the name of Jesus Christ! According to YOUR will, it is done in Jesus' name!

If you are a sinner, please pray the following prayer and receive Jesus Christ into your life this very moment. He's waiting for you.

Father God, I come before you now in the name of Jesus Christ. I confess that I am a sinner and I want to be saved from my sins. I do not want to continue in this life of sin. Jesus Christ is Your Son and He died for my sins. Father, You raised Him from the dead!

Jesus, I want You! I really need YOU right now and forever! I invite You into my heart right now. I accept You into my heart right now. Come in and live in me now!

I believe that You have come into my heart and life!

Father, all these things I have asked and prayed in the name of Jesus Christ! Thank You for these and all other blessings! I will live for You and You alone! In Jesus Christ's name I pray, Amen!

I AM SAVED!

ABOUT THE AUTHOR

Shane Wall has ministered the Word of God Internationally for over 30 years.

Shane Wall was born and resides in Orangeburg, S.C. with his wife Jasmyne. He is the founder and pastor of The Feast of the Lord in Orangeburg, SC. He began ministering the Word of God at fifteen years of age.

He is the author of the book, What Are You Doing After the Dance? He recorded a Gospel CD entitled, Conversations with God. Each song on the CD is written by Shane Wall and reveals sentiments shared by God and by His children.

He formed The Church FM (Fellowship Ministry) for pastors and their congregations to benefit from the experience he's gained as a leader in the church and in the community.

CONTACT

Shane Wall
P. O. Box 2005
Orangeburg, SC 29116

(803) 395-0190

www.understandingnow.com
www.facebook.com/pastorshanewall
www.twitter.com/shane_wall
www.linkedin.com/pub/shane-wall/7/6a/972